P9-CFB-110

The Culturally Proficient School

*An Implementation Guide
for School Leaders*

Second Edition

Randall B. Lindsey

Laraine M. Roberts

Franklin CampbellJones

CORWIN
A SAGE Company

CORWIN
A SAGE Company

FOR INFORMATION:

Corwin

A SAGE Company

2455 Teller Road

Thousand Oaks, California 91320

(800) 233-9936

www.corwin.com

SAGE Publications Ltd.

1 Oliver's Yard

55 City Road

London EC1Y 1SP

United Kingdom

SAGE Publications India Pvt. Ltd.

B 1/I 1 Mohan Cooperative Industrial Area

Mathura Road, New Delhi 110 044

India

SAGE Publications Asia-Pacific Pte. Ltd.

3 Church Street

#10-04 Samsung Hub

Singapore 049483

Acquisitions Editor: Dan Alpert

Associate Editor: Kimberly Greenberg

Editorial Assistant: Heidi Arndt

Production Editor: Amy Schroller

Copy Editor: Amy Rosenstein

Typesetter: C&M Digitals (P) Ltd.

Proofreader: Annie Lubinsky

Indexer: Scott Smiley

Cover Designer: Glenn Vogel

Permissions Editor: Karen Ehrmann

Copyright © 2013 by Randall B. Lindsey, Laraine M. Roberts, Franklin CampbellJones

All rights reserved. When forms and sample documents are included, their use is authorized only by educators, local school sites, and/or noncommercial or nonprofit entities that have purchased the book. Except for that usage, no part of this book may be reproduced or utilized in any form or by any means, electronic or mechanical, including photocopying, recording, or by any information storage and retrieval system, without permission in writing from the publisher.

Printed in the United States of America.

Library of Congress Cataloging-in-Publication Data

This book is printed on acid-free paper.

SUSTAINABLE FORESTRY INITIATIVE

Certified Chain of Custody
Promoting Sustainable Forestry
www.sfiprogram.org
SFI-01268

SFI label applies to text stock

13 14 15 16 17 10 9 8 7 6 5 4 3 2 1

The Culturally
Proficient School

Laraine M. Roberts

This edition of *The Culturally Proficient School* begins with a note of sadness with the loss of our beloved friend and co-author, Laraine M. Roberts. We have had the opportunity to know and work with Laraine on many projects over the years, none more special than the two editions of this book. Laraine contributed much to us, just as she did to all who knew her. Although we could memorialize her in many ways—her scholarship, her love of family, her commitment to the ideals of educational equity—we choose to highlight her delightful sense of humor in order to hear her laughter once again.

Laraine loved humor and often punctuated her presentations with a joke or two. We are indebted to Laraine and our friend Marilyn Nebenzahl for providing us with one of Laraine's favorites:

Penguin Story

A man drives to a gas station and has his tank filled up. While doing this, the clerk spots two penguins sitting on the back seat of the car. He asks the driver, "What's up with the penguins in the back seat?"

The man in the car says, "I found them. I asked myself what to do with them, but I haven't a clue."

The clerk ponders a bit then says, "You should take them to the zoo."

"Yeah, that is a good idea," says the man in the car and drives away.

The next day the man is back at the same gas station. The clerk sees the penguins are still in the back seat of the car.

"Hey, they're still here! I thought you were going to take them to the zoo!"

"Oh, I did," says the driver, "and we had a great time. Today I'm taking them to the beach."

It is so nice to hear Laraine's melodious laugh once again.

Contents

Foreword

FIRST EDITION

School administrators facing issues of accountability, diversity, and no child left behind expectations may benefit from a work that presents a process by which to respond to these challenges. The process is not a quick fix, recipe, or the answer to serious issues. However, the process does address questions such as the following: How culturally proficient am I? How culturally proficient is my school? What are the stages by which I and my school become culturally proficient? How can I tell if we are making progress? How is this proficiency related to the relationships I need to develop and sustain? How do these relationships and our Cultural Proficiency relate to our accountability to our constituents? How is Cultural Proficiency linked to the improvement of student performance?

The Culturally Proficient School focuses on Cultural Proficiency as a concept that calls for school leaders to respond to the challenges facing them in their schools and communities. The issue of differences in the school organization is dealt with from the standpoint of the leaders. These differences are conceived as cultural, which call for some response that may consist of six stages: cultural destructiveness, cultural incapacity, cultural blindness, cultural precompetence, cultural competence, and Cultural Proficiency. These stages range from purging cultures to honoring differences among cultures. Leader behaviors, values, and attitudes are dealt with to illustrate how culturally proficient leaders succeed in bringing about improvement in student performance.

This book is a friendly invitation to consider and try certain strategies to improve the culture of schools and to become culturally proficient. A valuable contribution of this work is that the responsibility for the betterment of schools is firmly lodged on the leadership of the organization as well as others. Cultural Proficiency is a type of relationship that exists between the leader and others but also between members of the organization and community. How that relationship is developed, nurtured, and strengthened is systematically presented. As an instructional strategy, the use of the Maple View case and the practical "how to" chapters are particularly effective. The case presents a picture of reality we have all experienced, whereas the "how to, can do" chapters reflect a spirit of optimism and well-crafted strategies to help leaders and others to develop Cultural Proficiency. This is not a simple step-by-step description of assuming attitudes, behaviors, and values advocated by the authors as consisting of Cultural Proficiency. Instead, it is a work that demands reflection, experimentation, and insight into organizational and personal aspects of associating with one another.

Inasmuch as the authors express modest intentions of this book, the value of this work for me lies in the clarity of the relationship between the case, the conceptual framework, and the call for leadership and organizational purpose. It is rare to find a work that is pragmatic, data based, and theoretically sound with the potential to not only impact the preparation of school leaders but also elevate the possibilities for our schools and youth.

Flora Ida Ortiz
University of California, Riverside

Foreword

SECOND EDITION

Achieving Cultural Proficiency within schools is a possibility and a key component of educational reform in the United States. As educators everywhere face the challenges of leading schools with significant student achievement gaps, it is incumbent upon them to be courageous and address concerns related to culture. Clearly, school and district leaders, who sustain an unwavering focus on curriculum, instruction, and assessment, can transform struggling schools and districts into high-performing academic institutions that make a difference for all students. However, this keen focus must also include an understanding of culture and its complex dimensions as essential elements of a culturally competent school.

As school leaders undertake the arduous task of creating equitable opportunities for all students, crucial questions arise. What is the role of school leaders in transforming schools into culturally proficient cultures that break through persistent achievement gaps? How do school leaders address the complexities and challenges associated with Cultural Proficiency in ways that are constructive and nonconfrontational? How do school systems build leadership capacity to combat biases that hinder teaching and learning for all students? These questions have implications for self-reflection, introspection, and collaboration among staff members within the school system and with institutions of higher education.

The Culturally Proficient School provides educators with multiple opportunities to consider these questions using real-world cases to frame conversations. Understanding the value of diversity and the need to preserve the cultural dignity of students, Lindsey, Roberts, and CampbellJones present a framework of strategies that sensitively guides school leaders through the phases of the Cultural Proficiency Continuum. They provide practical tools for enhancing the Cultural Proficiency of individuals and school organizations. Readers are invited to reflect upon their own beliefs, assumptions, and personal experiences about culture as they examine real-life cases from the field. Self-reflections are discussed within the context of the six stages of the Cultural Proficiency Continuum: cultural destructiveness, cultural incapacity, cultural blindness, cultural precompetence, cultural competence, and Cultural Proficiency.

As I experienced the reflective activities and ensuing spirited conversations propelled by *The Culturally Proficient School,* I was compelled to explore the values, beliefs, and principles that form my professional behavior. This purposeful reflection allowed me to analyze my own level of competence in addressing the systemic inequities present within school systems. I was left feeling hopeful about my capacity to empower other leaders in creating culturally proficient schools. The authors also provide meaningful professional development activities, supported by scholarly research. These activities provide a common set of experiences for schools and districts that seek to embed culturally competent norms and practices within their cultures. District leaders, school leaders, teacher leaders, parent leaders, and community leaders have an opportunity to break through historical divisions within school systems and make a profound difference in the world.

The increasing cultural diversity among students attending urban schools challenges educators to provide quality and equitable education for every student. To address this challenge effectively, leaders must be culturally proficient themselves. Transforming schools into inclusive and rigorous learning environments requires a notable level of fearless, yet strategic, leadership, which breaks through the barriers to creating a culturally proficient school. As leaders grapple with this challenge, ripples of hope will transcend obstacles and improve schools.

The advancement of cultural competence should be an integral part of any school district's improvement process; and then, and only then, can a school district successfully raise achievement for all students and be transformed.

Sid Salazar, EdD
Assistant Superintendent Instructional Support Services Division
San Diego Unified School District

Acknowledgments

It has been almost 20 years since we first read Terry L. Cross, Barbara J. Bazron, Karl W. Dennis, and Mareasa R. Isaacs's seminal monograph *Toward a Culturally Competent System of Care* (1993). The framework they developed continues to be a beacon for sensitive and responsive ways to meet the needs of culturally and ethnically diverse clients. For us it serves as an effective tool for guiding preschool through Grade 12 schools, colleges, and universities to be attentive to the needs and goals of our diverse constituencies.

This second edition is now one of 13 Cultural Proficiency books that has emanated from the initial books authored by Kikanza Nuri-Robins, Raymond D. Terrell, Delores Lindsey, and Randall B. Lindsey. We are most appreciative to them and the other authors who have joined in constructing in-depth work that demonstrates how to apply Cultural Proficiency in school settings. Cultural Proficiency is setting a new standard for educators willing to educate all children and youth. In this edition, we draw from the concepts developed by Cross and adapted by the Cultural Proficiency authors and add the voices of our colleagues in PK–12 schools, colleges, and universities.

This book is about voice. The three of us have, cumulatively, several decades of experience with PK–12, college, and university education. During our careers, beginning in the early 1960s, public education has expanded to serve ever-widening sectors of society. At best it has been uneven, and at worst it has contributed to the disparities in our society. Our goal in writing this book is to provide a handbook for the many educational leaders we encounter who are seeking opportunities to have meaningful conversations about developing culturally proficient practices.

We are deeply indebted to our many generous colleagues who have supported us in this work. There are many people represented in these pages as the voices to whom we have listened and from whom we have learned. They are the voices of teachers, teacher aides, administrators, parents, community members, and college and university faculty members who have an abiding interest in our schools being ever more successful in serving the academic and social needs of our children and youth. We have labored with one another in the creation of this new edition. Our labor ends with a sense that we have only begun the process of telling the story of what Cultural Proficiency looks like in practice.

A special note of appreciation to Delores Lindsey, who has been a coach, mentor, and informer through both editions and has provided critical feedback for both form and content. Delores's contributions are extensive and have contributed mightily to a book of which we are proud. We are truly grateful for the loving enthusiasm, friendship, and critical feedback that Brenda CampbellJones provided as this project moved from conception to near-completed drafts. We appreciate James Crow for his dedicated and tireless editing of our first edition, which has made constructing this book a smooth process. Delores, Brenda, and Jim are professional partners, as well as partners for life, in this important work of serving the needs of our diverse communities.

We are blessed to have Corwin's continuing interest in and support for our work. Dan Alpert, our editor and advisor, knows and supports the work of equity and access and is a tremendous ally in creating a socially just society. The support of Heidi Arndt, our associate editor, keeps us focused and on track, for which we are most appreciative. The production team at Corwin is most impressive in their commitment to high standards at all phases of production. Finally, we appreciate you for your interest in our work and trust that it will serve you well in your professional endeavors.

About the Authors

Randall B. Lindsey, PhD, is Emeritus Professor, California State University, Los Angeles, and has a practice centered on educational consulting and issues related to equity and access. Prior to higher education faculty roles, Randy served as a junior and senior high school history teacher, a district office administrator for school desegregation, and an executive director of a nonprofit corporation. All of Randy's experiences have been in working with diverse populations, and his area of study is the behavior of white people in multicultural settings. It is his belief and experience that too often, white people are observers of multicultural issues rather than personally involved with them. He works with colleagues to design and implement programs for and with schools, law enforcement agencies, and community-based organizations to provide access and achievement.

Randy and his wife and frequent coauthor, Delores, are enjoying this phase of life as grandparents, as educators, and in support of just causes that extend the promises of democracy throughout society in authentic ways (randallblindsey@gmail.com).

Laraine M. Roberts, EdD, served as Senior Research Associate at WestEd in San Francisco. Her work centered on educational leadership, organizational culture, and school and district development and improvement. In addition to leading educational research projects, she designed and facilitated leadership development programs for superintendents, district administrators, and school principals. In all her work, her goal was to influence changes within the structures of schools and the practices of educators that result in meaningful learning experiences and academic success for all students. Her experiences as an educator included classroom teaching, school and district administration, professional development, curriculum development, and university teaching.

Franklin CampbellJones, EdD, has spent his entire career as an educator. He has served as high school social science and reading teacher, assistant principal, program director, state director for the California School

Leadership Academy, and university professor at California State University, Los Angeles, and Rowan University in Glassboro, New Jersey. He continues to chair and serve on dissertation committees and is a contributing faculty member at Walden University. Franklin has been fortunate to give keynote addresses and professional seminars in Thailand, The People's Republic of China, Guam, and Canada. School systems throughout the United States consult with him about equitable change using the lens of Cultural Proficiency. He is Vice President of *CampbellJones & Associates*. He enjoys independent research and scholarship related to organizational change that advances equity in schools and communities (www.campbelljones.org).

Introduction to the Second Edition

This second edition of *The Culturally Proficient School* has provided us, Franklin and Randall, the opportunity to write together again and to share with you what we are learning from and about schools engaged in the work of Cultural Proficiency. We began the journey of this edition with Laraine and remember her with a memorial in the Dedication.

Corwin continues to be supportive of our writing and exemplifies a publisher committed to socially just practices. The second edition incorporates our learning from working with schools, educational agencies, and organizations engaged in educating their staff members and clients. We also continue to learn from colleagues like you who have used previous editions to deepen your own understanding of Cultural Proficiency in service of our schools and related organizations. We share with you some of these learnings in this edition.

Since the publication of this first edition in 2005, we have been pleased with three constant responses to *The Culturally Proficient School*. First, we consistently meet educators and community partners who, after having read the case-story vignettes, indicate that we must have modeled the case story on their school-community. Usually, we had never visited their school or community but were gratified to see the relevance of the issues addressed in the book. Second, we receive very supportive comments about the design and presentation of the material. Feedback we receive can be grouped into two categories: opportunities to reflect and engage in dialogue throughout the book, and conversation and lab protocols updated in Chapters 7 and 8 of this edition. Third, we consistently receive positive feedback that we have fused practical, on-site applications with prevalent theoretical and research literature that addresses issues of oppression, education, and leadership in an integrated approach.

Although we've worked hard to retain the integrity of the first edition, we've made the following improvements to this edition:

- A conceptual framework for Cultural Proficiency is presented in Table II.1, Introduction to Part II.
- The content and vignettes have been updated and expanded.
- The format has been reorganized to present a progression of topics to ease reading and use of reflection and dialogue activities.
- A Book Study Guide has been added to the Resources section as an aid for professional learning.
- A matrix has been added to the Resources section that describes how to use other Cultural Proficiency books.

Conceptual Framework

Developing the conceptual framework shaped our thinking about the book and led to revisions designed to make the work increasingly relevant, accessible, and effective. The conceptual framework demonstrates the interrelationship of the Tools of Cultural Proficiency. The Introduction to Part II presents and describes the conceptual framework, and Chapters 3 through 6 provide detailed descriptions of the Tools of Cultural Proficiency.

Updated Content and Case Story

The world has continued to change since the first edition was published, and we place a high value on keeping the content and vignettes relevant and forward looking. We take pride in our continuing involvement with PK–12 schools, educational agencies, and organizations across the United States and Canada engaged in their members' professional learning. This edition continues to present the characters in the case story informed by our experiences and to present issues relevant to today's schools and agencies. The content of the vignettes reflects what we are learning about personal values and behaviors and organizational policies and practices that support educators being effective in our schools and related agencies. The vignettes and the content of the text are supported with relevant academic and research citations.

Revised Format

This format is designed for ease in reading. Part I sets the context for achievement gaps as the focus of the book and for the fictionalized community of Maple View as a case-story setting. Part II guides you into understanding the Tools of Cultural Proficiency for personal and organizational applications. Part III is structured for use as professional learning about topics of effective conversation and leadership for learning.

Resources Section

The Resources section of the book provides two useful tools to enhance ongoing learning—a matrix of how to use other Cultural Proficiency titles and a Book Study Guide:

- The Book Study Guide is intended for use in deepening individual understanding of the content and for use in collegial professional learning.
- The Breakthrough Questions Guide is designed to support the use of effective questions and the related activities in Chapter 7.
- The matrix lists other Cultural Proficiency books and the essential questions that guided the books' development. The guiding questions may guide your deeper learning and your professional growth as well.

As you will see in the matrix, 14 books on Cultural Proficiency are now available or in production. Each of the Cultural Proficiency titles has a

Table I.1 'Apps' of Cultural Proficiency

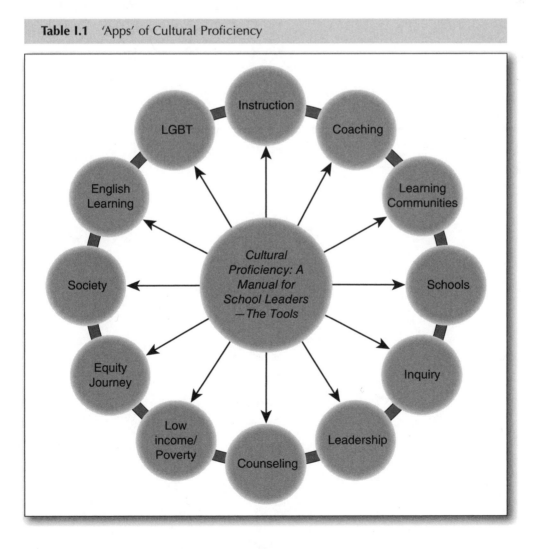

distinct application of the Tools of Cultural Proficiency, and the matrix is organized to inform you of which book(s) may be appropriate for your use. The table, the "Apps" of Cultural Proficiency, is a pictorial representation of the Cultural Proficiency books. The original and core book, *Cultural Proficiency: A Manual for School Leaders,* now in its third edition, presents our most detailed description of the Tools of Cultural Proficiency. The books radiating from the manual also present the basic tools in an applied manner relating to the books' intent (e.g., instruction, coaching).

We are fortunate to have colleagues much like you who have contributed to the improvement of this edition of *The Culturally Proficient School.* Educators in PK–12 schools, colleges/universities, educational organizations, and agencies engaged in educating their staff members and clients throughout Canada and the United States have been generous in describing how this book enhances their own learning and professional development with colleagues.

Randall B. Lindsey

Laraine M. Roberts

Franklin CampbellJones

Part I

Introduction—Cultural Proficiency and the Achievement Gap

The United States and Canada are at the precipice of making democracy work in ways not conceived by the founders of our respective countries. Since World War II, our countries have embarked on a mission to provide a comprehensive education to all students—a mission that has been uneven across the varied demographic groups served by our schools. The early part of this century is now witnessing strong efforts to overcome past discrimination and focusing on educating all children. Whether the impetus to educate all children and youth in ways not envisioned a generation ago is from moral persuasion, economic motivation, governmental prodding, or a combination of all, the fact remains that our countries are seeking to educate all students. Excuses grounded in deficit thinking about our students' socioeconomic origins, race, ethnicity, gender, gender identity, sexual orientation, ableness, or faith are no longer acceptable. Gaps in student achievement among demographic groups of students are now consistent topics of discussion in our schools and communities.

Although achievement gaps are neither new nor unusual and, in fact, are historical and well documented (Oakes, 1985; Perie, Moran, & Lutkus, 2005), what is new, and unusual, is that for the past decade, discussions about access and achievement gaps have moved beyond the walls of the schoolhouse and into mainstream communities. Whereas two and three generations ago, unscrupulous real estate agents and financial institutions "redlined" communities in ways that provoked white and middle-class flight away from schools and communities of color, thereby establishing *de facto* districts of privilege and districts of neglect, today's schools are compelled to teach all students. The excuse that students' cultural and demographic characteristics are handicaps to learning are being eroded but not without resistance in many quarters.

Schools continue to seek programs that respond to often deeply ingrained resistance to educating all students to high academic levels. Over the past two generations, several authors have worked diligently in support of equitable access and outcomes for PK–12 students. Educators such as James Banks (1994), Jim Cummins (1990), Paolo Freire (1970), Geneva Gay (2000), Henry Giroux (1992), bell hooks (1990), Jonathan Kozol (2007), Henry Levin (1988), Cameron McCarthy (1993), Sonia Nieto (2004), Myra and David Sadker (1994), Mara Sapon-Shevin (1993), Theodore Sizer (1985), Robert Slavin (1990), Christine Sleeter and Carl Grant (2007), Cornel West (1993), and Anne Wheelock (1992) are among the many who have and still do press forward in nudging and pushing schools and agencies that fund them to view equity as a path to equality.

The chapters in Part I are designed to support your learning about achievement gap issues. Chapter 1 presents and discusses achievement gaps in ways that invite you and your colleagues to reflect on the culture of your school as well as the cultures served by your school. You will have opportunity to think and discuss with colleagues the applicability of No Child Left Behind mandates and Common Core State Standards to the manner in which you work and interact with your students and the communities from which they come. Chapter 2 presents the fictional school district of Maple View, which is a composite of the many schools and school districts with which we have worked across the United States and Canada. Maple View might serve as a vision for your school or district. However you experience the Maple View story, the dilemmas and opportunities will be familiar. The "voices" will be voices that you have heard. The Maple View chapter provides an important context to which you can apply the Tools of Cultural Proficiency presented in Part II.

Enjoy your journey—you will learn about your assumptions, both the positive and the negative ones; you will find reflection to be a tool of comfort and confidence building; and you will experience dialogue as a means for developing a team-based approach to systemic change that benefits all of your students.

Culture Frames Achievement Gaps

We must first comprehend the fact that children—all children—come to school motivated to enlarge their culture. But we must start with their culture . . . for they are rich in assets. As teachers, we enter their world in order to aid them and to build bridges between two cultures.

—Eugene Garcia (1999, p. 8)

GETTING CENTERED

We assume that in picking up and beginning to read this book, you are seeking to improve your school in ways that serve all students equitably. With that assumption in mind, we suggest you begin this journey of experiencing culturally proficient schools by considering several questions:

- If schooling were to build bridges between and among the cultures that currently exist in your school, what might that look like?
- If schooling were a means for enlarging one's own culture through meaningful interactions with people from other cultures, what might that look like?
- From your experience, what are some of the assets that children and youth bring to schools that can serve as bridges to their increased academic success?

Use the space that follows to record your thinking and questions that might be occurring to you.

_____

_____

_____

_____

Quite possibly your thoughts and questions involved educators searching for ways to work more successfully with students who represent the varied cultural, ethnic, linguistic, religious, sexual orientation, gender diverse, and socioeconomic cultures within our diverse society. Cultural and social diversity is certainly not a new issue for us as humans. Diversity has always existed and, yet, we remain challenged by it. The burgeoning complexity of our times provides opportunities for us as educators to embrace ways that value the cultures of our students as assets on which to build their educational experiences.

Failure to embrace students' cultures as assets gives rise to deficit-based thinking and places far too many students in danger of being excluded from the benefits and opportunities of being well educated. This book addresses the challenges that grow out of the demographic and cultural array of students we serve in our schools by offering an approach to education that embraces diversity and responds to it in ways that acknowledge and esteem cultural differences while simultaneously valuing and supporting similarities in a process of additive rather than subtractive acculturation (Ogbu, 1992). The approach we propose is Cultural Proficiency, which offers both educators and their students knowledge and understanding of how to interact effectively with people in their environments who are culturally different from them. The Cultural Proficiency model we describe derives from the work of Terry Cross in a monograph he wrote for health care practitioners, *Toward a Culturally Competent System of Care* (Cross, 1989; Cross, Bazron, Dennis, & Isaacs, 1993).

CULTURAL PROFICIENCY

In the third edition of our initial book, in what has become a book series, Cultural Proficiency is described to be "a model for shifting the culture of the school or district; it is a model for individual transformation and organizational change. Cultural Proficiency is a mindset, a worldview, a way of being assumed by a person or an organization for effectively describing, responding to, and planning for issues that arise in diverse environments. For some people, Cultural Proficiency is a paradigm shift *from* viewing cultural difference as problematic *to* learning how to interact effectively with other cultures" (Lindsey, Nuri Robins, & Terrell, 2009, p. 4).

Culturally proficient leaders strive to demonstrate behaviors aligned with their espoused values that lead to effective communication with their colleagues, students, parents and community members. At the school and district levels, culturally proficient leaders promote practices aligned with policies that bring about effective interactions among educators, students, parents, and community members. When leaders and their organizations are intentionally on a journey to Cultural Proficiency, conflict and change are embraced as natural consequences of people coming together and are not to be feared. Change and reform are valued allies in providing equitable educational opportunities for all children, youth, and adult learners served by the school.

CULTURAL PROFICIENCY MANAGES CHANGE

In our work with the Tools of Cultural Proficiency, several questions arise quite appropriately—"Cultural Proficiency? What is that?" "What does it mean?" Some of the educators with whom we work ask these questions when we introduce the term. Quite often, their follow-up questions reveal their real concerns about expected behaviors: "What does it look like in practice?" Commonly, the unspoken concerns are, "Will I be expected to change my behavior?" "Will I have to act differently?" and "What if I feel uncomfortable?" Other educators immediately begin to find ways to integrate new practices into their interactions with students, colleagues, parents, and members of the community. They want to work more effectively with students who represent the many cultural groups within our diverse society. While educators search for quick fixes that do not exist, others understand the systemic nature of cultural change in an organization and begin the complex work of transforming their schools and districts into inclusive communities. Members view acknowledgment and respect for diverse groups as appropriate and worthy goals for their organizations and work toward improved education for all students.

Make no mistake about it, organizational change is challenging and requires a leader's persistent systemic reinforcement. Indeed, Edgar Schein, in *Organizational Culture and Leadership* (1992), emphatically argues that "the only thing of real importance that leaders do is create and manage culture and . . . the unique talent of leaders is their ability to understand and work with culture" (p. 5).

Educational leaders intent on transforming their schools and districts into pluralistic, inclusive organizations must first be willing and able to look deeply into their own tacit assumptions about the diverse students with whom they work and examine their expectations about those students' achievement potential. Leaders also must identify and pursue effective ways to educate all their students successfully, using strategies that both acknowledge and respond to the students' varied cultural backgrounds.

This book offers ideas, tools, and processes to serve as a guide for leaders through the complex and challenging cultural transformation of their organizations. Again, Schein's (1992) seminal work illuminates this idea:

> I believe that cultures begin with leaders who impose their own values and assumptions on a group. If that group is successful and the [leader's] assumptions come to be taken for granted, we have then a culture that will define for later generations of members what kinds of leadership are acceptable. The culture now defines leadership. But, as the group encounters adaptive difficulties, as its environment changes to the point where some of its assumptions are no longer valid, leadership comes into play once more. Leadership now is the ability to step outside the culture that created the leader and to start evolutionary changes that are more adaptive. This ability to perceive the limitations of one's own culture and to develop the culture adaptively is the essence and ultimate challenge of leadership. (pp. 1–2)

In this new edition of our book, our goal is to share with you what we are learning from our work with leaders who recognize the access and academic achievement disparities in our schools and who have made a commitment to leverage their leadership to create and manage schools and districts that function at high levels of cultural and social interaction among diverse groups. These leaders acknowledge that diversity is far more than racial or ethnic differences, and their actions reflect a sincere intent to understand and respond to all the cultural and demographic groups in their schools and districts—particularly groups other than the ones they represent. These leaders also recognize that their and their colleagues' responses and reactions to cultural diversity have a profound influence on what students learn and how they learn it. Culturally proficient educational leaders have learned that responding to and reacting to *difference* manifest in several ways, which range from cultural destructiveness to Cultural Proficiency. The range of these responses comprises the points of the Cultural Proficiency Continuum (Lindsey, Nuri Robins, & Terrell, 1999, 2003, 2009):

- *Cultural destructiveness:* negating, disparaging, or purging cultures that are different from your own
- *Cultural incapacity:* elevating the superiority of your own cultural values and beliefs and suppressing cultures that are different from your own
- *Cultural blindness:* acting as if differences among cultures do not exist and refusing to recognize any differences

- *Cultural precompetence:* recognizing that lack of knowledge, experience, and understanding of other cultures limits your ability to effectively interact with them and beginning to engage in a willingness to learn
- *Cultural competence:* interacting with other cultural groups in ways that recognize and value their differences, motivate you to assess your own skills, expand your knowledge and resources, and, ultimately, cause you to adapt your relational behavior
- *Cultural Proficiency:* committing to life-long learning for self and your school, committing to actions that are in the best interest of all students, and advocating for the underserved

Educational leaders can create school cultures in which Cultural Proficiency is a dominant value. Pluralistic and democratic schooling must be our goal. Schools in which these ideals take root and flourish require leaders to both model and expect behaviors that are consistent with them. Through our work, we have observed that schools begin to change when their leaders recognize the disparities that exist in their schools and then intentionally raise issues of bias, marginalization, preference, legitimization, privilege, and equity. By choosing to face these issues and grapple with them directly to understand their effects on student learning, these leaders are moving themselves as well as their schools and districts toward culturally proficient practices. In contrast, for leaders who choose to turn away from these issues as if they have no effect on student learning, then, of course, nothing will change. In these circumstances, the achievement gap between students who have been historically well served and the students who have not been will continue to grow and deepen. As educators, we can choose to contribute to access and achievement gaps, or we can choose to change the contextual conditions that support the inequities that created and perpetuate the academic achievement gap.

OUR INVITATION TO YOU: FROM NCLB TO COMMON CORE

As you read this book, we invite you to consider new or alternative perspectives on the many ways we can educate the diverse groups of students in our schools and classrooms. The approach we propose is a focused strategy that significantly and persistently addresses the problems of educational inequity. We firmly believe that education leaders must mobilize a sustained and coherent strategy that challenges the dominant deficit and at-risk characterizations of some students. An inclusive, pluralistic, and instructionally powerful learning environment offers the real likelihood that all students will be well-educated and successful learners.

The No Child Left Behind (NCLB) Act of 2001 ushered in the 21st century with new hope that all demographic student groups would be served in ways that would close access, achievement, and education gaps. Even the 2014 deadline seemed hopeful given the funding sources behind the mandate. Intervention programs sprung up almost overnight it seemed in response to the mandate's "scientific-research" requirements for education interventions in support of reading and math achievement. Districts across the nation began to see important achievement gains by student groups who had not experienced success prior to the gap that had been exposed by NCLB. Following the reauthorization of the Elementary and Secondary Education Act (ESEA), popularly known as NCLB, the second round of ESEA came on the horizon with Barack Obama's presidency in 2009. The vision of all students reaching high levels of achievement once again came into question with the assessment deadline of 2014 from NCLB seemingly unattainable. The U.S. Department of Education then focused federal education resources toward a national curriculum called the Common Core State Standards (CCSS) that would be realized through Race to the Top (RttT), the U.S. Department of Education's version of NCLB revised.

As states applied for RttT funding, their educational leaders also moved forward in writing and approving CCSS, a requirement for RttT funding. The CCSS were unveiled in 2010 and as of this writing have been adopted by all but five states. The design and implementation plans moved forward quickly with common assessments, common curriculum, and common texts and resource materials. As state departments of education and local school districts and schools position themselves to implement the CCSS by 2014, numerous questions face educators who use equity-based models, such as Cultural Proficiency, as a lens to examine their work:

- In what ways will we use the "education gap" data that we collected and analyzed from NCLB?
- In what ways will we incorporate our "lessons learned" from our NCLB conversations about closing our education gaps?
- Why will CCSS serve us in ways NCLB did not?
- Why will CCSS provide opportunities to address issues of equity and inequity?
- Is CCSS the "what," "how," or "why" of educating all learners?
- In what ways might CCSS provide access to college and careers to all learners in ways that have not happened before?
- What's different about the educators with the implementation of CCSS that will make this "reform" a transformative change in schools and school districts?

Answers to the inescapable "why" question are wrapped around the concept of equity. Educational leaders who pursue the goals of pluralistic and democratic schooling act intentionally by responding to the "why" question with the belief that all children and youth not only have the capacity and right to learn, but also they are learning about themselves and others at every moment.

Democratic educators recognize that most U.S. schools are very successful educating the students for whom our schools were designed, and they recognize that this is a narrow cluster of students who represent mainstream European American individualistic values that predominate U.S. public schools. As you read the Guiding Principles of Cultural Proficiency in Chapter 4, you will note they are equity-focused and inclusive of all students in our schools. Democratic educators understand the imperative that all students must receive the caliber of education they need to fully contribute to and sustain our democratic society. Also, they remain skeptical of the conventional explanations given for the achievement gap—that there is something wrong with the student, their parents, or their culture—and are fully committed to identifying and removing deterrents to academic achievement among undereducated students.

Perspectives as to causes of the achievement gaps are many, but three predominate and overlap in our schools:

● Significant segments of society and educators hold deficit-based perspectives that children and youth from low socioeconomic or conditions of poverty, children and youth of color, and children and youth who are English learning students are not succeeding in our schools because of cultural deficiencies.

● Another perspective held by some members of society and educators is that systemic oppression, such as racism and exclusion, is responsible for the undereducation, if not the miseducation, of children and youth from low socioeconomic and impoverished conditions, children and youth of color, and English learning children and youth. This perspective describes how systemic oppression, as forms of exclusion and marginalization, obstruct the educational progress of some students while simultaneously benefitting and propelling the progress of other students.

● A third perspective held by some members of society and educators describes children and youth for whom our schools were designed and for whom they function well as also experiencing deficits. However, their deficits are rarely discussed. Students from mainstream ethnic, social, and economic groups often develop a worldview of privilege and entitlement that isolates them from learning how to interact effectively in a multicultural society (Delpit, 1995; Kovel, 1984; Ladson-Billings, 1994; Lindsey & Daly, 2012; Nieto, 2000, Quezada, Lindsey, & Lindsey, 2013; Terry, 1970).

These perspectives recur throughout this book and are used to help educators develop an understanding of how they and their schools can progress from recognizing "deficit-based" perspectives that predominate their schools, to recognizing systemic oppression, and to developing culturally proficient leadership behaviors and organizational practices. This book offers leadership strategies to explore the how and why some children and youth fail in our schools and why others succeed. We invite you on this journey to find the will and means for our schools to serve the educational needs of all students.

THE "WHY" OF THIS BOOK

Our intent is to weave a tapestry of strategies with an understanding of organizations as dynamic and culturally adaptive systems that can significantly support transformative learning, what educational journalist Gene Maeroff (1999) describes as "altered destinies." A central tenet of this book is that effective leaders act with intentions informed through a personal transformation of taking responsibility to lead in a way that addresses the educational needs of all students (Delpit, 1995; Ladson-Billings, 1994; Reeves, 2000, Shields, 2010).

Chapter 2 presents the composite case story of Maple View. With this chapter, you will be introduced to a school district and a set of people, many of whom may appear quite familiar to you. The Maple View case story is important in that it gives "voice" to the many equity issues we face in schools today. Please acquaint yourself with the story and the persons who comprise the story; doing so will make your learning in Parts II and III ever more active and enable you to apply associated learning to your professional practice and to that of your school or district.

2 The Importance of Culturally Proficient Leadership

Giving priority to what matters is the path of risk and adventure, but I also believe that the institutions and culture that surround us are waiting for us to transform them into a fuller expression of our own desires . . . We also have the capacity and maturity to live a life of service and engagement, rather than the primary pursuit of entitlement and interests that focus on ourselves.

—Peter Block (2001, p. 7)

THE CASE: MAPLE VIEW

Maple View had been a growing suburban city that expanded rapidly until the recession that began in 2008 hit with impactful consequences. Only a few years ago, the city's population was 30,000 and included mainly middle-income and lower salaried workers and their families. The new Pine Hills Estates development of "executive" homes was just beginning to grow and add upper income residents, but recessionary pressures caused growth to slow. These executive professionals commute from several large high-tech corporate headquarters and research and development centers in the area. The city's Planning and Economic Development Department estimates that the Pine Hills Estates residents represent approximately 5% of the population. Middle-income residents have shrunk from approximately 65% to 50% of the city's population, and they serve as its major economic base. The low-salaried, service-industry-worker population has swelled from 23% to 33% of the population, and the "working poor" and the unemployed population—who are dependent on government assistance for many basic services and family needs—has increased from 7% to 12%.

Though the city's population has remained flat during the recession, there are signs that a slow recovery is on the way, and it is projected that population growth will be more diverse than in the past. The city's chamber of commerce has adopted the following slogan: "Maple View: Our Diverse City Is Growing to Meet Your Needs!" The key stimulus for this increase has been a projected resurgence of housing development across economic segments. On the West Side, the developer of the Pine Hills Estates has resumed building an additional 150 large, expensive homes, many around a newly developed golf course. Much of this new construction has taken over land previously used for agriculture, including a popular cut-flower farm that employed 40 people throughout the year, with additional temporary workers during high-volume times. The West Side had been a growth area for new middle-class housing tracts that drew new residents to Maple View from more congested and densely populated urban centers, and all signs are for that growth to resume. Three new, moderately priced developments have added 275 well-constructed but small homes that are selling quickly because of their pricing when compared with prerecessionary housing costs. In addition, because of the master plan developed with the support of the volunteer service group, Leadership Maple View, the Planning and Economic Development Department submitted a housing development proposal to the U.S. Department of Housing and Urban Development. Maple View successfully won a federal grant and built 186 subsidized apartments and 30 low-cost houses on the East Side of the city.

The city's resurgent growth is exerting pressure on its social institutions, such as schools, public transit, and hospitals, while at the same time stimulating economic development of its business community. New retail shopping centers, banks, chain restaurants, movie theater complexes, and national big-box stores such as Lowe's, Home Depot, Target, and Petco have opened on the West Side. In addition, a new upscale shopping "galleria" has replaced the old mall next to the state highway. A state-of-the-art movie multiplex is near completion next to the galleria, along with four new upscale restaurants. The city's planners are also developing construction specifications for a civic center complex to include a new city hall, police department, and performing arts center. The specifications are being reviewed in public meetings, and once local and state tax revenue projections are completed early next year, a plan for competitive bidding will be announced.

The East Side, with the exception of the new low-cost housing units, is not experiencing much outside economic development. The major state highway divides Maple View into two separate communities, and few East Side residents go beyond this boundary unless they are venturing to one of the large discount chain stores just across the highway. The "old" downtown, as people in the city's business community refer to it these days, is no longer the economic center of the city. Many of the original stores have gone out of business. However, a revitalization led by local residents is underway, with new businesses, stores, and restaurants opening in the old buildings. The revival effort is contributing to a vibrant local economic community that offers products and services reflecting the lifestyles and preferences of the East Side residents. In marked contrast to local East Side revitalization efforts, the city's Planning and Economic Development Department is neither investing in new development nor refurbishing the old neighborhood parks and public buildings on the East Side, and the area is taking on a shabby look of disrepair in some sections. Quite a few East Side homeowners in the Maple Street and Main Street sections are justifiably proud of their vintage houses and have invested a great deal of time and effort in restoring and maintaining them. In fact, many young professional couples from outside the community are choosing to purchase these older homes and live in East Side neighborhoods rather than in the newly built homes on the West Side.

The large University Medical Center is located near the northwest city limits of Maple View. This 450-bed teaching hospital is an important source of employment for the city's residents—from doctors to janitors and from administrators to laundry workers. The hospital's chief administrative officer, Dr. Jack Bradley, has been involved in community development efforts in Maple View for the 15 years that he has worked at the hospital. As a pediatrician, he is witness to the changes in Maple View's population firsthand. In the past few years, he has treated an increasingly diverse group of young patients and also has observed the results of economic, cultural, social, and educational disparities. Dr. Bradley lives with his family in an older section of Maple View on the East Side. As the volunteer project director for Leadership Maple View, Dr. Bradley has made it his personal mission to develop leadership capacity across his diverse community. He spearheaded the leadership group that developed the proposal for federal funding of low-cost housing in the city. He is currently working with Dr. James Harris, Director of Academic Programs at the Tri-Cities Community College (TCCC), on a new leadership effort to involve East Side residents in an innovative bilingual-bicultural medical assistant training at the hospital. The new program will be called "Culturally Proficient Medical Assistance Training."

TCCC is on the southeastern edge of the city, approximately five miles from the old downtown center. The two-year college serves 1,900 students from Maple View and two nearby cities. Dr. Harris and other administrators at the college are concerned about the disappointing statistics they have just received as part of a report on their students' transfer to four-year colleges and universities. Only approximately one third of their entering students complete the university transfer credits and go on to complete a four-year degree program. The administrators at TCCC worry that many graduates from area high schools are entering the college poorly prepared to succeed in the rigorous academic program required for transfer to a four-year degree program. Dr. Harris fears that these students not only enter TCCC poorly prepared but also have no idea how to access sufficient support and assistance to become fully prepared. He believes that these students grow to fault themselves and accept blame for not having the "cultural capital" to successfully navigate the educational system. Dr. Harris has made an appointment with Dr. Sam Brewer, the newly appointed superintendent of the Maple View School District, to discuss this issue and find ways to support the students. Dr. Harris is going to miss the recently retired superintendent, Dr. Barbara Campbell, but is well aware of Dr. Brewer's sterling reputation as principal of Pine Hills High School and is eager to begin this next chapter for the Maple View community.

MAPLE VIEW SCHOOL DISTRICT

The public school system in Maple View has a great reputation. The district consistently scores in the top 15% of districts throughout the state in the statewide standardized testing program. As a result, almost all the families in the city send their children to their local, neighborhood schools. The Maple View School District serves 11,200 students from PK–Grade 12. The ethnic composition of the student enrollment reflects the racial, ethnic, and cultural diversity of the city:

37% White

24% Latino/a (first, second, and third generation from Central America, South America, and Mexico)

21% Asian (third and fourth generation from China and second and third generation from Korea and the Philippines)

14% African American

2% Native American

2% Pacific Islanders (first and second generation from American Samoa)

Twelve percent of the student population is in special education programs, and 10% of the students are learning English as a second language. Across the district, students speak 12 different primary languages.

Dr. Sam Brewer, in his second year as superintendent, and the members of the district's school board, along with other district administrators, recently worked together at an administrative retreat to create a statement of their vision for the district. They published the following statement: "The Maple View School District commits its effort and resources to provide a high-quality education for all students that enables each one to achieve or exceed high academic and performance standards." Dr. Brewer, or "Sam" as he prefers to be called by colleagues, is not completely satisfied with the negotiated statement but knows that he can work with it. However, he is pleased with the collaborative process used to develop the vision statement.

The impending growth in student enrollment is a major concern for the superintendent and the school board. In the past year, they have dealt with thorny issues of reassigning students, locating portable classrooms on school sites, and investing in new construction. Throughout this challenging period, Dr. Brewer has kept his focus on issues of equitable distribution of resources, fair and just allocation of high-quality educational experiences, and the acceleration of achievement for undereducated and underperforming students.

The school board members are elected at-large and serve the entire district rather than a particular geographical area or constituency. In the recent elections, very few East Side residents have sought office, and no one from the East Side neighborhoods has served on the board for at least six years. Eighteen months ago, the five current board members asked Dr. Brewer, then principal at Pine Hills High School, to consider assuming the position of district superintendent. The previous superintendent, Dr. Campbell, had retired after 10 years in the position. Sam agreed, and the board's vote to approve his contract was unanimous; they assured him that he had their full support.

Projected construction and development within the district's boundaries, especially on the West Side, will result in significant revenue growth from developer fees and real estate assessments. Dr. Brewer views these funds as resources that can be used to equalize resources across the district. He is troubled by poor student performance results in the schools in East Side neighborhoods, and he knows firsthand that those schools have fewer fully qualified teachers than schools on the West Side. He also knows that many of the teachers at the East Side's Maple View Elementary School and Maple View Middle School are newly hired teachers, and some of the high school teachers are not fully prepared to teach the subject matter for their assigned grade levels or departments. Sam is dedicated to extending Barbara's vision to transform these schools into high-performing learning communities like the schools on the West Side.

MAPLE VIEW: THE PEOPLE

The story of the city of Maple View, its school district, and its residents provides an illustration of why culturally proficient leadership is important. The fictional characters in the case are composites of the many schools and school districts with which we have worked across the United States and Canada. The characters in this case story face many of the challenges that will confront you as a leader searching for ways to integrate culturally proficient values, attitudes, and behaviors into your leadership practices. Because schools do not exist in isolation of the communities they serve, the Maple View case story allows us to present a contextualized setting in which a variety of situations occur and in which the members of this community are willing and motivated to reveal themselves and their thinking because they have problems to solve. The process of learning and solving the problems faced by characters in this case story makes known the cultural transformation that takes hold in their schools and alters the outcomes of its members. This case presents only a small sampling of the kinds of issues that might surface in an educational setting such as the Maple View School District. Nonetheless, the case offers an opportunity to analyze the actions of the characters and to learn why culturally proficient leadership is so important.

You will meet many of the citizens of Maple View in your reading of this book. The Resources section of this book lists the people in the sequence in which they appear in the book. People are identified by their roles in the school or community.

LEADERSHIP ACTION THAT MATTERS

In the chapters that follow, the Maple View case unfolds as a story of leadership that matters. The leaders—administrators, teachers, parents, and community members—of Maple View tackle challenges such as equitable opportunities and resources to learn, culturally sensitive instruction, expectations and assumptions about student performance, and willingness to learn new ways of being with students. As educators and parents work together to resolve these problems, they learn to view their individual and collective behavior through the lens of Cultural Proficiency. They learn to ask, "Will this decision result in a more culturally proficient organization?"

Each chapter offers an opportunity to learn more about the phases of development toward Cultural Proficiency and to consider why it is important and how you might integrate culturally proficient practices into your daily leadership practice. The Essential Elements of Culturally Proficient practice provide standards as benchmarks against which you can calibrate your leadership behavior. To begin, use the scale presented in the following section to assess your openness to the work you will undertake in this book.

INVITATION: ASSESS YOUR RECEPTIVITY

To read this book with purpose, we invite you to assess your receptivity to its content. The Cultural Proficiency Receptivity Scale will support you in your learning. Cultural Proficiency is deep, personal introspective work one undertakes before attempting to influence the behavior of others. Chapters 2 through 5 present the Tools of Cultural Proficiency designed to support you in self-examination of your own values and behaviors and to enable you to examine the policies and practices of your school and its grade levels or departments.

Our belief is that personal leadership evolves from the inner work experienced by effective leaders. Leader effectiveness occurs when leaders are clear with themselves and others about what they value and believe (Banks, 1999; Covey, 1989; Heifetz, 1994; Sergiovanni, 1992, Shields, 2010). In discussing the inner work of principals, Fullan (2003) states, "The principal with a moral imperative can help realize it only by developing leadership in others" (p. xv).

The Cultural Proficiency Receptivity Scale is a nonscientific instrument designed to guide you through a process of self-reflection. The concepts in this scale derive from the information you will be reading in Chapters 2 through 5. We urge you to read each of the statements and indicate your level of agreement on the 1–7 Likert scale. A response of 1 indicates strong disagreement, and a response of 7 indicates strong agreement. When you have finished reading the book, we encourage you to return to the scale and reassess your levels of agreement. The purpose of this scale is to introduce you to important concepts in a manner that personalizes the content of the book. Please note, the scale is not a test and is not intended for that use.

CULTURAL PROFICIENCY RECEPTIVITY SCALE

I believe that all children and youth learn successfully when informed and caring educators assist them and make sufficient resources available to them.

Strongly Disagree		Agree			Strongly Agree	
1	2	3	4	5	6	7

I want to do whatever is necessary to ensure that the students for whom I am responsible are well-educated and successful learners.

Strongly Disagree		Agree			Strongly Agree	
1	2	3	4	5	6	7

I am committed to creating both an educational environment and learning experiences for our students that honor and respect who they are.

Strongly Disagree		Agree			Strongly Agree	
1	2	3	4	5	6	7

I am willing to ask myself uncomfortable questions about systemic oppression (e.g., racism), cultural preferences, and insufficient learning conditions and resources that are obstacles to learning for many students.

Strongly Disagree		Agree			Strongly Agree	
1	2	3	4	5	6	7

I am willing to ask questions about systemic oppression, cultural preferences, and insufficient learning conditions and resources that may be uncomfortable for others in my school or district.

Strongly Disagree		Agree			Strongly Agree	
1	2	3	4	5	6	7

I believe that all students benefit from educational practices that engage them in learning about their cultural heritage and understanding their cultural background.

Strongly Disagree		Agree			Strongly Agree	
1	2	3	4	5	6	7

I believe that all students benefit from educational practices that provide them with hope, direction, and preparation for their future lives.

Strongly Disagree		Agree			Strongly Agree	
1	2	3	4	5	6	7

It is important to know how well our district serves the various cultural and ethnic communities represented in our schools, and it is also important to understand how well served they feel by the educational practices in our schools.

Strongly Disagree		Agree			Strongly Agree	
1	2	3	4	5	6	7

It is important to know how the various cultural and ethnic/cultural communities represented in our schools view me as an educational leader and to understand how well my leadership serves their expectations.

Strongly Disagree		Agree			Strongly Agree	
1	2	3	4	5	6	7

Our district and schools are successful only when all demographics and cultural groups are improving academically and socially.

Strongly Disagree		Agree			Strongly Agree	
1	2	3	4	5	6	7

Cultural discomfort and disagreements are normal occurrences in a diverse society such as ours and are parts of everyday interactions.

Strongly Disagree		Agree			Strongly Agree	
1	2	3	4	5	6	7

I believe that lack of cultural understanding and historic distrust can result in cultural discomfort and disagreements.

Strongly Disagree		Agree			Strongly Agree	
1	2	3	4	5	6	7

I believe we can learn about and implement diverse and improved instructional practices that will effectively serve all our students.

Strongly Disagree		Agree			Strongly Agree	
1	2	3	4	5	6	7

I believe we can use disaggregated data to understand more precisely the achievement status of all students in our schools and that we can use that information to identify and implement effective instructional practices for each of them.

Strongly Disagree		Agree			Strongly Agree	
1	2	3	4	5	6	7

As a leader, it is important for me to be able to communicate across cultures and to facilitate communication among diverse cultural groups.

Strongly Disagree		Agree			Strongly Agree	
1	2	3	4	5	6	7

Review your responses, compute your total score, and record it here
_____. (The range of scores is from 15 to 105.)

What does your score mean? Are you highly receptive? Are you not receptive? Are you "middling"? We ask that you resist using your initial score as anything more than a baseline of information. This book is designed to guide and support your personal journey to becoming more effective in cross-cultural situations. Accordingly, this instrument is one tool among several reflective tools in this book that you will use in the development of a personal leadership perspective for making a difference in your school community.

When you have completed the book, we invite you to return to your responses and to analyze them to support you in your journey to Cultural Proficiency. If you are reading about Cultural Proficiency for your own personal growth, reflect on your responses and be prepared to revisit them after completing the book. At that time, you will be able to assess what you have learned about yourself, about personal change, and about complex organizational change. If you are reading this book as part of a professional development activity with colleagues or as part of a university course, discuss your responses with others and explain why you responded as you did to the several items. Then, as with the focus on personal growth, you will want to revisit your responses after completing your work and reflect on your learning about personal and complex change.

GOING DEEPER

Now that you have completed the two chapters in Part I, what resonates for you? In what ways does information in these chapters support your prior knowledge about schools, your school, or you as an educator? What questions are surfacing for you about your practice as an educator or your school in service to all students? Please use the space below to record your thoughts.

_____

_____

_____

_____

Part II introduces the Tools of Cultural Proficiency. Chapter 3 guides you to learn how Barriers to Cultural Proficiency obstruct and limit school change. This very important chapter juxtaposes "-isms" issues (e.g., racism, sexism) with issues of privilege and entitlement. When you have completed Chapter 3, you will learn that the two seemingly diametrically opposed issues of -isms and privilege/entitlement are in reality two halves of a whole that create and reinforce one another.

Part II

Introduction— The Tools of Cultural Proficiency

An Inside-Out Change Process

Cultural Proficiency is an interrelated set of tools to guide you in making changes in your practice and in working with colleagues to guide changes in your school's policies and practices intended to narrow and close access and achievement gaps. Chapters 3 through 5 have been designed with four goals in mind. Upon completion of these chapters, you and your colleagues who have been engaged in the study of this book will be able to:

- Describe barriers to Cultural Proficiency you may have experienced or observed that impede students' access to equitable academic and social outcomes in your school.
- Describe how the Guiding Principles of Cultural Proficiency serve as core values for your personal, professional, and your school's organizational/cultural values and behavior.
- Describe unhealthy and healthy educator values and behaviors as well as school policies and practices, and plot them along the Cultural Proficiency Continuum.
- Describe and use the five Essential Elements of Cultural Competence as standards for your personal and professional behavior and your school's formal policies and nonformal, prevalent practices.

THE CONCEPTUAL FRAMEWORK IS A GUIDE

The conceptual framework provides the "big-picture view" of the manner in which the Tools of Cultural Proficiency interrelate with one another. You may want to tab Table II.1 so you can easily refer to it to as you read, reflect on, and discuss the content of Chapters 3 through 5. We suggest reading Table II.1 from the bottom up to see that we have a choice—to have either deficit-based barriers or the asset-based guiding principles as core values and foundations for our work as educators. From Chapters 3 and 4, you will learn that the lower portion of the conceptual framework illustrates the manner in which cultural assets form the basis for professional and school-wide core values. Recognizing and understanding the tension that exists for people and schools in terms of barriers versus assets prepares you to better serve the students in your classroom, school, and district.

Chapters 5 and 6 illustrate the upper portion of the conceptual framework and provide the most visible aspects of the framework—the very language we use to discuss our students and their cultures, the extent to which our policies and practices embrace our students' cultures as assets, and professional standards to guide our practice.

If this is your first book on Cultural Proficiency, you are about to embark on a journey of self discovery that will deepen your good work, provide insight to areas of growth for you and your school, and make you a more responsive educator in service of your students and their communities. Should this not be your first book on Cultural Proficiency, you will deepen your knowledge and skills. Our frequent conversations with colleagues who have read more than one of our books have revealed that they appreciate our "apps" approach. Since publishing *Cultural Proficiency: A Manual for School Leaders* in 1999, we have published 12 more titles, each of which is an application of the Tools of Cultural Proficiency first described in the Manual.

Table II.1 The Conceptual Framework for Culturally Proficient Practices

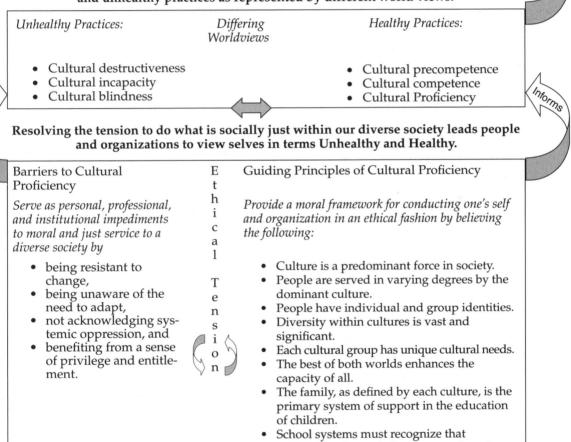

The Five Essential Elements of Cultural Competence

Serve as standards for personal, professional values and behaviors, as well as organizational policies and practices:

- Assessing cultural knowledge
- Valuing diversity
- Managing the dynamics of difference
- Adapting to diversity
- Institutionalizing cultural knowledge

The Cultural Proficiency Continuum portrays people and organizations who possess the knowledge, skills, and moral bearing to distinguish among healthy and unhealthy practices as represented by different world views:

Unhealthy Practices:	*Differing Worldviews*	*Healthy Practices:*
• Cultural destructiveness • Cultural incapacity • Cultural blindness		• Cultural precompetence • Cultural competence • Cultural Proficiency

Resolving the tension to do what is socially just within our diverse society leads people and organizations to view selves in terms Unhealthy and Healthy.

Barriers to Cultural Proficiency	Ethical Tension	Guiding Principles of Cultural Proficiency
Serve as personal, professional, and institutional impediments to moral and just service to a diverse society by • being resistant to change, • being unaware of the need to adapt, • not acknowledging systemic oppression, and • benefiting from a sense of privilege and entitlement.		*Provide a moral framework for conducting one's self and organization in an ethical fashion by believing the following:* • Culture is a predominant force in society. • People are served in varying degrees by the dominant culture. • People have individual and group identities. • Diversity within cultures is vast and significant. • Each cultural group has unique cultural needs. • The best of both worlds enhances the capacity of all. • The family, as defined by each culture, is the primary system of support in the education of children. • School systems must recognize that marginalized populations have to be at least bicultural and that this status creates a distinct set of issues to which the system must be equipped to respond. • Inherent in cross-cultural interactions are dynamics that must be acknowledged, adjusted to, and accepted.

Reprinted from *Cultural Proficiency: A Manual for School Leaders, 3rd Ed.* by Randall B. Lindsey, Kikanza Nuri Robin, and Raymond D. Terrell. Thousand Oaks, CA; Corwin.

 # 3 Overcoming Self-Imposed Barriers to Moral Leadership[1]

Do we have the will to educate all children?

—Asa Hilliard (1991, p. 31)

GETTING CENTERED

Upon reading Dr. Hilliard's epigraph that opens this chapter, what thoughts, reactions, and questions does his query evoke for you? Take a moment and think about his question to us. Use the space to record your response.

_____

_____

_____

_____

MAPLE VIEW DISCOVERS WHAT IT CARES ABOUT

The Maple View Elementary School leadership team members have decided to have Dr. Brewer coach them on their Cultural Proficiency

---

[1]AUTHORS' NOTE: For purposes of consistency, material in this chapter is adapted from an earlier Cultural Proficiency book—Randall B. Lindsey, Kikanza Nuri-Robins, & Raymond D. Terrell. (2009). *Cultural proficiency: A manual for school leaders* (3rd ed.). Thousand Oaks, CA: Corwin.

journey. Dr. Brewer initiated this process about two weeks ago and is very interested to find out how they are individually and collectively involved with creating a school culture committed to educating all children. He recognizes that this venture is not without risk, and he realizes this is a worthwhile risk if the Maple View School District is to be serious about educating all children and youth.

Dr. Brewer offered opening comments to the leadership team meeting: "Our state legislature enacted the Public School Accountability Act in 1999. How many of you were teachers, counselors, or administrators before that time?" Many participants raised their hands in acknowledgment. He noted that even though the staff and faculty were largely a veteran force, several were new to education. "Since that time our country has experienced national efforts to address achievement gaps in the forms of No Child Left Behind (2001) and Race to the Top (2009). It is important that we recognize that these legislative efforts launched an accountability movement that, though discontinuous across our country, has provided an opportunity to democratize education in ways that seemed unfathomable a generation ago."

He continued, "Let me guide you in making a personal connection to the reality of the impact of accountability. How many began your education careers since 1999?" Several people raised their hands. "As a school district, we have been analyzing disaggregated data as required by our state's Public School Accountability Act and No Child Left Behind since 2002." Most nodded their heads, indicating their agreement with her. Dr. Brewer was aware that for many veteran administrators and teachers, learning how to use student data had been a new and often time-consuming process. For those who became educators since 2000, accountability measures were part of their everyday reality. However, both veteran and new educators recognized that in those early years, many schools resisted the new accountability measures. "Of those of you who raised your hands, how many were aware of the disparities that the disaggregated data have revealed?" Along with the participants, Sam Brewer raised his hand. He looked across the group and asked, "What does that say about us? We have been aware of these disparities for years but waited for the state and national governmental leaders to require us to get moving!"

Sam and the leadership team came face to face with the reality of the quote in the epigraph for this chapter: "Do we have the will to educate all children?" Asa Hilliard (1991) posed this question to our profession more than 20 years ago. However, we continue to struggle to answer it. The question invokes a sense of moral purpose or responsibility. The question carries with it a veiled accusation—that we have not been educating all children and, indeed, maybe we do not have the will to do so.

The achievement gap had been one of the worst kept secrets in the education community. It is, too often, the undiscussable issue that educators grudgingly have acknowledged but often continue the struggle to find courage to explore in meaningful ways. The accountability movement provided the opportunity to examine disaggregated student achievement data by demographic groups. This has shed light on facts that we educators had hidden in aggregated student results. This illumination is revealing the genuine disparities and inequities that had been accepted by educators as "the way things are" or "We're doing pretty well, considering. . . ." Long overdue in this ongoing discussion was admitting that there is an achievement gap. With accountability, those excuses are now "off the table," and educators are beginning to concede the situation is an ethical and moral imperative (Fullan, 1991, 2003, 2010; Sergiovanni, 1992). In truth, we have been complicit in the undereducation, if not the noneducation, of our children and youth from low-socioeconomic, Native American, African American, Latino, English-learning, and special education groups.

In Chapter 6, we describe how culturally precompetent and culturally competent educators use the moral authority of their school leadership positions to successfully confront issues of oppression. We recognize that the word *oppression* is emotive for some people, and readers may react negatively to our use of this word to describe educational policies and practices. However, the disparities that are maintained in our educational system are, indeed, oppressive and serve to maintain the position, power, and privilege of the dominant group. Most assuredly, the term oppression is an appropriate descriptor for the fact that issues of undereducation continue to exist generation after generation.

Our experiences have revealed that many educators are stuck in trying to combat the continuing effects of "-isms"—racism, ethnocentrism, sexism, heterosexism, and ableism. The roadblock that people must circumvent often begins with what we refer to as "doing their own work." First, a person must understand his or her own feelings about uncomfortable information. Second, the individual must take actions that are in the best interest of the students. This "feeling-to-action" connection either impedes or facilitates action.

Reflective Activity

When you hear or use words such as *racism, ethnocentrism,* or *sexism,* what are the thoughts that come to mind?

_____

_____

_____

_____

What feelings do the "-isms" words generate in you?

_____

_____

_____

_____

Returning to Maple View Elementary School, we find members of the school leadership team continuing to struggle. Joan Stephens and Connie Barkley were commiserating about their most recent Cultural Proficiency session. Joan was struggling with her deep, emotional reactions to the session. She knew that Connie had sponsored the session and felt that she could share with Connie some of her concerns and questions:

Joan:	Connie, you know from the very beginning, way back when Dr. Brewer first started talking about the journey to Cultural Proficiency, that I have been in full support of this effort. But, after our session yesterday, something is really bothering me.
Connie:	What is it, Joan? How can I help you?
Joan:	Well, I guess mostly by just listening.
Connie:	Is it fair to ask "hard, maybe difficult" questions?
Joan:	Oh, that's scary. What do you mean?
Connie:	Well, maybe I am anticipating your comments, but I am struck by your using the phrase about "being in full support of this Cultural Proficiency effort." And then you attached the notorious "but." Is that where you want to begin?
Joan (somewhat deflated):	Well, yeah. I am stunned by how quickly you went to the heart of the matter. Connie, I listened to the speaker, I read the book, I engaged in the activities, but I cannot escape feeling blamed.
Connie:	Describe for me what you mean by "feeling blamed."
Joan:	Arrrgggghh! Sometimes I feel angry; other times I feel guilty. However, I know those feelings are not productive, so I just sit on them.
Connie:	No, you don't, Joan. You internalize them to anger, guilt, or frustration. I am never sure which it is.
Joan:	What do you mean?

Connie: Joan, we have been friends and colleagues for several years, and I think I know a little about you as a person. Frankly, Joan, you seem to want the Cliffs Notes version of Cultural Proficiency. I think Dr. Brewer has really tried to help us see that Cultural Proficiency isn't our latest project; it's a lens through which we can view our current work and our interactions with our students. Our values and beliefs are most evident in the assumptions we have about our students.

Joan: Connie, I think I understand that. But what do you mean about my wanting the "Cliffs Notes version of Cultural Proficiency"?

Connie: Remember what our facilitator said yesterday: We must understand systems of oppression and their impact. For example, think about racism and its effects on people at both a personal and institutional level.

Joan: Yeah. Okay.

Connie: Let me know if this makes sense to you. Racism negatively impacts both the victims and perpetrators. Let's take the historical periods of slavery and Jim Crow. African Americans were obviously impacted due to loss of personal liberty and being confined, at best, to second-class citizenship. At the same time, the rest of the population, mostly white, lost moral bearing in allowing such practices to persist. Does that make sense, Joan?

Joan: Unfortunately, yes, it makes a lot of sense. But I don't know what to do with the information and how that impacts the here and now of our school and my classroom.

Connie: Principally, Joan, until we confront legacies of racism, it interjects destructive energy into the system—like the school or a classroom. By understanding this double-edged impact, we are more able to see and feel the effects of oppression on our students and ourselves and work to combat it. We are more prepared to ask ourselves hard questions about our own assumptions and their effects. It's not easy to question our intentions and the intentions that are unwittingly institutionalized in our organizations. And yet, this is the only way we can change things. I particularly resonated with Dr. Brewer's comment that one of the major impediments to school reforms is that those who have benefitted from current practices don't see a need to change the way they do business. In other words, the system serves them well, so must something must be wrong with the students or their culture.

Joan: Let's suppose you are accurate and, believe me, I am beginning to see the situation in ways you describe them, then, why do I feel this way?

Connie: Your feelings are natural and normal, Joan, and a hard question you might ask is: "What are you willing to do, and how are you willing to change to create the best learning environment for all students at this school?" Joan, we can't be the observers in this change process. We are the leaders. Our feelings can be indications of being on the verge of deeper and more powerful learning.

Joan: You make my being stuck sound like resistance or denial.

Connie: Just imagine, Joan, if you have the feelings you are describing, what it is like for the students who are not succeeding at this school? And, you're a parent, Joan. Think about how your students' parents must feel when they don't see value added for their children being in our schools. They also may feel angry, guilty, and frustrated by the circumstances they are caught up in.

This conversation between Joan and Connie illustrates the authors' belief and experience that too often, educators stand on the sidelines, observing oppression and its disastrous results rather than becoming personally involved with them. As Dr. Brewer found out from his questions to his educator colleagues, we have known of the achievement gap for decades and as a profession have done alarmingly little about it (Perie, Moran, & Lutkus, 2005). As educational leaders, the questions for us are as follows:

- How did we arrive at these disparities in our schools?
- How do the forces of entitlement and privilege affect our profession?
- What are these feelings of anger and guilt, and why do I have them?
- What are our responsibilities as school leaders?

Reflective Activity

What educational disparities for students do you see in your school or district?

_____

_____

_____

_____

Please describe your reactions to the disparities in your school.

_____

_____

_____

_____

ENTITLEMENT AND PRIVILEGE AS EDUCATION HISTORY

At the dawn of the 20th century, a comprehensive education was an opportunity not available to most citizens. In one century, our country has progressed from offering a comprehensive public education to a small portion of the population to making public education available to most people. In the early 21st century, the promise and the possibility still exist, but the promise is unfulfilled. Well-informed educational leaders may be the linchpins of our democracy, serving our citizens in ways not envisioned by our counterparts a century ago.

During the past century, as this country matured, greater access to a comprehensive public education resulted from economic and legal pressures. The economic growth of the country demanded an increasingly better-educated workforce. However, women and people of color had to rely on judicial and legislative actions to participate fully in public education as a means for gaining entry into the economic mainstream of our country. School desegregation, Title IX, and Public Law 94–142 are examples of legislative and judicial steps used to gain access to educational opportunities.

However, access did not guarantee a quality education. Recently, and often because of the pressures exerted by judicial decisions and legislative actions, schools have begun to address the needs of diverse populations. The accountability movements that are in place in federal and state initiatives expect, for the first time in our history, all students, irrespective of their cultural backgrounds, will achieve a standards-based education. As controversial as these initiatives may be, they stand in a long line of modern educational initiatives. The most prominent of these initiatives was the _Brown v. Topeka Board of Education_ (1954) decision that led to school desegregation. Desegregation efforts since the 1960s have been preoccupied with the thorny issues of physical access to school campuses and have only recently become involved with both the input and the output of the educational process. Prekindergarten through Grade 12 schools have experienced segregation, desegregation, and integration, and they still struggle to provide an effective education to all sectors of society. Today's school leaders are in a unique position to become advocates for all children and youth to receive a comprehensive education and also to help build communities that affirm goals of academic and social success.

During the latter part of the 20th century, terms such as *diversity* and *multiculturalism* described a complex society that had always existed but was rarely acknowledged by the dominant culture. These changes are pushing us beyond unquestioned acceptance of the prevailing view of early 20th-century white male scholars who predominated in establishing the policies and practices of U.S. public education (Bohn & Sleeter, 2000; Sheets, 2000). The achievement gap is the lingering evidence of historical inequities and a persistent challenge to educational leaders.

Once people understand the concepts of entitlement and privilege, they must also have the will to make the ethical and moral choices implicit in such an understanding. One of the common denominators for all systems of oppression is that people lose rights and benefits because of discrimination against them. Privilege and entitlement occur when rights and privileges denied to one group of people accrue to others. These rights and privileges are often taken for granted in unrecognized and unacknowledged ways. For example, if you cannot vote because of your skin color and I can vote because of mine, functionally I have two votes—mine and the one denied to you. Similarly, if I have access to an enriched educational experience that involves higher thinking skills and you are assigned, year after year, to low-level direct/drill instruction, I will be better prepared than you to perform well on any measure of academic success placed before me.

TRANSFORMATIVE LEADERSHIP

As you will read in Chapter 6, moving from being culturally precompetent to being culturally competent entails a shift in thinking. A component of this shift in thinking is to understand the concepts of entitlement and privilege and their relationship to systems of oppression. Racism and other forms of oppression exist only because the dominant group benefits from the continued practices. Culturally competent educational leaders shift their thinking and are intentional in understanding not only the negative consequences of oppression but also the benefits of those same systems.

We must become "the change we want to see" (Gandhi, 2002). Mahatma Mohandas K. Gandhi's words let us know that we are at the heart of creating the world we envision. Dismantling systems of oppression, such as racism, requires transformation that necessarily involves the deconstruction of power in both personal and institutional forms. Weick (1979) holds that organization is a myth and that "most 'things' in organizations are actually relationships tied together in systematic fashion" (p. 88). In other words, we invent social organizations through our interactions with one another. Cultural destructiveness and Cultural Proficiency are similarly invented ways of organizing our social interactions. The choice is ours: We can continue to perpetuate historical racism and inequity, or we can lead our organizations to historical levels of effectiveness and achievement. It is all invented: A human invention is created by those within the system called "school" (Zander & Zander, 2000).

Leadership that leads to change can be characterized as transactional, transformational, or transformative. Shields (2010) describes each type of leadership:

- Transactional leadership involves a reciprocal interaction in which the intention is for agreement and both parties benefit from the decision. For example, decisions in which faculty and principal agree to twice-monthly meetings that focus on improving literacy skills for all students are transactional leadership behaviors.
- Transformational leadership focuses on improving organizational effectiveness. Continuing with the example of improving student literacy, faculty agrees with principal to engage in professional development for instructional improvement that focuses on literacy literature and skill development.
- Transformative leadership recognizes that gaps in student literacy are found in inequities that are generational and correlated with students' demographic groupings. Continuing with the literacy examples, faculty and principals collaboratively challenge practices that marginalize students and press for equitable academic access and outcomes (pp. 563–564).

Culturally proficient educational practices, and leadership, are exemplified through the standards described in the culturally precompetent, culturally competent, and culturally proficient environment illustrations in Chapter 6. Culturally proficient education exists within the context of our moral authority as educational leaders. Making the shift from culturally precompetent to culturally competent involves three aspects of our moral authority:

- Recognizing the dynamics of entitlement and privilege,
- Recognizing that our schools contribute to disparities in achievement, and
- Believing that educators can make choices that positively affect student success.

Cultural competence and Cultural Proficiency require a leadership perspective that involves an inside-out approach to personal and organizational change. Culturally proficient leaders redefine education in a democracy to be inclusive. These leaders focus on inequity and equity, regardless of who is benefiting from the current status. They focus on confronting and changing one's own behavior to learning from and how to serve the educational needs of new groups in the community, rather than how to change and assimilate members of target groups. Culturally proficient leaders expect criticism from influential people, and they operate in school districts by remaining centered on the moral value in our work as educators.

Coming to grips with privilege and entitlement is not without risk. The risk comes in questioning the process of public schooling and the institutional structures, policies, and practices that shape the learning processes in schools. Understanding privilege and entitlement and questioning the systems that support them require countering the legacy of history that has provided us with an educational system that is designed to educate some students and not others. Therefore, the hard question becomes: How have I benefited from the privilege and entitlement accorded to me as a result of my skin color, gender, social class, sexual orientation, age, and experience (Kovel, 1984; Tatum, 1999)?

Reflective Activity

What is entitlement or privilege?

_____

_____

_____

_____

How do you relate entitlement or privilege to "-isms," such as racism or sexism?

_____

_____

_____

_____

What are the risks involved for you as you transform your behaviors from cultural blindness to cultural precompetence?

_____

_____

_____

_____

FACING ENTITLEMENT: THE CONUNDRUM OF ANGER, GUILT, OR CONFIDENCE

Reactions to new information can often be discomforting. What was your reaction to the "hard question" in the preceding section? For many people, engaging in conversation about the topics of privilege and entitlement can generate an emotional reaction that ranges from anger to guilt. However, once people acknowledge and understand their very real feelings about this new learning, along with their recognition of the very real outcomes of privilege and entitlement, they are ready to begin learning to work more effectively with students and communities that are culturally different from theirs. This level of learning is empowering in that an individual can consciously direct his or her own learning and can continue discovering ways to be effective in working in cross-cultural situations (Cross, 1989; Freire, 1970, 1999). In the following vignette, you will see how two educators at Maple View Elementary School surface their feelings about entitlement and privilege:

Joan:	You know, I can take this discussion of racism and sexism, when the presenters are not so aggressive. Enough is enough!
Connie:	What do you mean by aggressive?
Joan:	Well, she just kept presenting information that is so very uncomfortable.
Connie:	But I do recall her asking about your reactions to the information and what your thoughts were. How is that aggressive? Do you think it would have been different for you if a white male had presented the information?
Joan:	Why would you ask me if I would have reacted differently had the presenter been white male?
Connie:	Well, as I see it, the presenter was not aggressive toward you. She merely presented ideas that you appeared to find upsetting.
Joan:	Upsetting? How the hell can you say that?
Connie:	Look at yourself right now—you have raised your voice, and you are pointing your finger right in my face. If that is not anger, I don't know what is!
Joan:	Listen, dammit, I resent people trying to make me feel guilty for something I did not create. I am fully prepared to be accountable for my actions, but I am not going to feel guilty for what "history" or "institutions" have done to anyone!

Educators such as Joan often become upset when discussing oppression and act out forms of anger or guilt or both. Figure 3.1 represents this range of reactions. People who have the ability to listen to the information and not accept the information as anger or guilt are confident they can use the information for constructive purposes.

Figure 3.1 Continuum of Reactions to Information About Oppression

Anger	Confidence	Guilt
X —————————————	X —————————————	X

Educational leaders who choose to remain angry or guilty when dealing with facts about the disparate success of students identified in demographic groups of race, gender, sexual orientation, social class, language acquisition, or special needs contribute to their own paralysis of inaction or inappropriate action. Figure 3.2 indicates that feelings of anger and guilt, although very different, are similarly dysfunctional for school leaders. The sense of frustration that arises from feelings of anger and guilt leads to inaction, which does not benefit underachieving students. Worse, the sense of frustration can lead to actions that are counterproductive for underachieving students. However, the educational leader who moves beyond his or her initial feelings to understanding the underlying issues of oppression is able to confront such issues with confidence. The leader's confidence is rooted in having made a moral decision to choose to use methods and materials that are effective for each demographic cultural group of students at the school.

Figure 3.2 Functional and Dysfunctional Reactions to Issues of Oppression

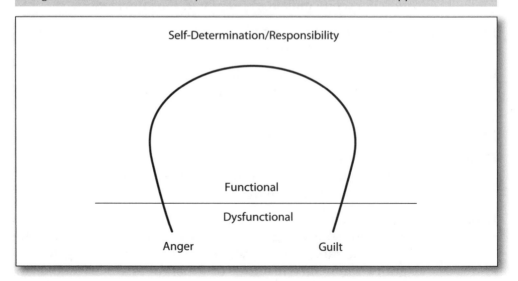

Moving Forward With Confidence. Making conscious, intentional choices is a mark of an educator who strives to improve his or her practice. Typically, for teachers and counselors, practice is improved by selecting and delivering curriculum and instruction that meet the needs of each and every demographic student group. For school administrators, practice is improved through marshaling resources in support of high-quality curriculum and instruction. Members of professional organizations and unions improve practice by ensuring that their core values address service to their students. At the policy-making level, improvement of practice involves school board members and district administrators setting and implementing policy that provides access for students from all sectors of the community. The confident person is proactive and asserts his or her needs, opinions, and views. This person also takes responsibility to facilitate others, particularly those who are silent, in understanding that their feelings may be an important avenue to new learning.

What is different about the members of these two groups of educators— those stuck in dysfunction and those who are able to move forward with confidence? The difference is the successful transition in a shift in thinking and disposition from cultural destructiveness, cultural incapacity, or cultural blindness to cultural precompetence and, eventually, cultural competence. The point between these two positions is what Gladwell (2000) termed the "tipping point." It is that point in time when a shift in thinking occurs. The shift in thinking occurs when the educational leader sees the behaviors of cultural destructiveness, incapacity, and blindness as inauthentic and inappropriate and is willing to shift to the arenas of possibility provided by culturally competent behaviors. The shift in thinking occurs when leaders recognize their stereotypic feelings and reactions and, through processes of reflection and dialogue, begin to examine their practice. You can see it in their eyes and hear it in their language; it is a moment of surprise, often expressed as a cognitive shift (Costa & Garmston, 2002; Schon, 1987). Through a cognitive process, the person actually begins to think in different ways. The evidence of the shift in thinking is observable in a person's newly stated beliefs and intentional actions as well as in physical and emotional reactions. This energy to do things differently and right is expressed through facial and posture changes.

REFLECTIONS ON ENTITLEMENT: A PINE HILLS ELEMENTARY SCHOOL CONVERSATION

Recognition of one's feelings or reactions is a first step to being able to constructively deal with issues of oppression in our schools and communities.

Let us return to the discussion between our two educator colleagues from Maple View School District's Pine Hills Elementary School. Joan is identifying how she has acknowledged her feelings and has begun to examine the deeper issues of how students are performing. She is becoming receptive to how she can make constructive choices to influence the learning of students:

Connie: It sure seems to me that you have personalized this entire presentation. I sat at the same table as you but had a very different reaction.

Joan: What do you mean?

Connie: I related the speaker's presentation to our current work on serving the needs of students identified as "underperforming." I must admit to moments of discomfort when she asked us to substitute "underserved" for "underperforming." Yes, I do feel a twinge when we realize schools are systems of oppression. But I have begun to focus on her comment, "When you feel that twinge of emotion, look to see if you are on the verge of deeper learning." For me, the deeper learning is involved with how can we become effective with students who are not being successful in our schools.

Joan: Well, if their parents don't even care . . .

Connie: Wait just a minute! You are feeding into just what the presenter described.

Joan: What do you mean?

Connie: By focusing solely on the parents, you are not considering the power and authority we have as educators. If we believe our students have the capacity to learn, then we can learn different and better ways in which to teach them. You do remember the EdTrust PowerPoint presentation, don't you? The one in which numerous schools with demographics just like ours are being very successful? It is about our taking responsibility to research, to find, and to use materials and approaches that work for our students and us.

Joan is being coached by Connie to look beyond her initial, personal reaction and examine her underlying assumptions about her students and their parents. Joan is on the verge of being able to exercise direct influence over how she views and works with her students and their parents. At this point, Joan, if she so chooses, will be more able and willing to begin examining her practice—the one thing over which she has total control—to see how she can work differently with her students. As Joan experiences this transition, she will feel more empowered. Her empowerment is her personal transformation.

Reflective Activity

What is your reaction to this section on anger, guilt, or confidence?

_____

_____

_____

_____

If you were to design a desired shift in thinking for yourself, what would it look like?

_____

_____

_____

_____

REFLECTIONS ON ENTITLEMENT: OPPRESSION, ENTITLEMENT, OR SELF-DETERMINATION AND PERSONAL RESPONSIBILITY?

The types of comments Joan made in the previous vignette are not new or surprising. They proliferate in the conversations that we hear in informal settings in schools at all levels (i.e., prekindergarten to university). People who make such comments do not seem to understand that people's experiences in our society vary greatly. For example, we have made presentations in which the demographics of schools and the inequities that exist are presented in quantitative detail. However, the same question arises almost every time. No amount of data can forestall it. The most compelling information on the underachievement of children from low socioeconomic backgrounds cannot derail it. The question is as follows:

> This is all well and good; however, how am I supposed to react when a student approaches me to contribute to a fund for Latino/ Latina scholarships? Now, I am a fair person. I came from a poor background. Why can't we just contribute to scholarships for all students of need?

Other times, it is in the following form: "As a school board member or administrator, it gets real tiring having these special-interest groups assail us at board meetings! Please, what are we to do with these groups? Why can't we treat everyone the same?" The following is another example:

> Why do we educators have to take the blame for students not achieving? Why doesn't anyone look at which students are the behavior problems in this school? Has it occurred to anyone that these are the kids who are low achievers? You don't think this is an accident, do you?

We do not doubt that the questions are often sincere and earnest. We do not doubt that these educators, who are gender diverse and of many ages and many cultural backgrounds, sincerely have these questions. However, one thing is inescapable: an underlying tension of anger, guilt, or frustration seems to accompany the question. Our response often begins with the following statement: "An important aspect of Cultural Proficiency is not so much what we learn about other people, but what we learn about our reactions to other people."

Our observation is that those who are privileged or entitled are often unwilling or unable to see the oppression that others experience (Bohn & Sleeter, 2000; Shields, 2010). Therefore, like Joan, when some people are confronted with new data or perspectives, their reactions are expressed as anger, guilt, or frustration. The inability to see how others experience our schools is very limiting. Several cultures acknowledge this limitation with maxims such as "You cannot understand me until you have walked a mile in my shoes." Not being able to see our entitlement limits our ability to move forward in our own learning to educate children from backgrounds different from ours to high levels of achievement. The damaging effects of racism and other forms of oppression are exceeded only by the unwillingness or inability of dominant society members to make the commitment to use one's entitlement to end oppression.

SELF-DETERMINATION AND PERSONAL RESPONSIBILITY: FROM FEELINGS TO ACTION

The feelings of anger, guilt, and self-confidence represented in Figures 3.1 and 3.2 have behavioral counterparts—namely oppression, entitlement, and self-determination/personal responsibility. Figure 3.3 represents a range of reactions, from oppression to entitlement, with self-determination and personal responsibility being the midpoint. In the same way that anger and guilt are opposite feelings and reactions, oppression and entitlement are opposite behaviors, and they too can lead to one being paralyzed and dysfunctional in making effective changes for our schools. The middle point of this continuum represents self-determination for those who are from historically oppressed groups, and it represents personal responsibility for those who are from privileged and entitled groups. The common denominator for both the oppressed and the entitled members is that they have constructive, functional choices to make and actions to take as educators.

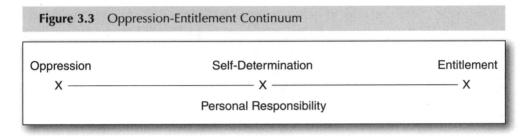

Figure 3.3   Oppression-Entitlement Continuum

Oppression is the consequence of racism, sexism, ethnocentrism, or heterosexism. Overt acts of oppression serve to deny the benefits of society to people based on their membership in a group. Throughout our country's history, visible acts of oppression in schools include tracking programs that precluded or limited mobility for specific ethnic or racial groups, chronic achievement gaps among groups, suspension and expulsion rates that are disparate among groups, and curricula that represent only dominant society. Less obvious, although no less pernicious, acts of oppression include lowered expectations, biased testing, and ethnocentric history and literature textbooks. Biased testing creates a reverse affirmative action. Ethnocentric textbooks have given the dominant society a mythical view of its role in the growth of this country and made all others invisible, exotic, or dehumanized. These practices are a significant part of our history and culture that, for too long, dominant society has tried to ignore. The very act of ignoring these issues is a choice reserved for only the entitled and privileged.

Self-Determination. Our experience is that when issues of oppression are raised, many of us who are from historically oppressed groups sometimes become agitated and angry that others in the group are either naive or resistant to hearing about our legacy of oppression. For people from historically oppressed groups, the struggle is to recognize systemic and systematic oppression and to commit oneself to self-determination. Possibly the ultimate oppression is for one to accept the notion that the system is so hopelessly racist, sexist, ethnocentric, or heterosexist that there is nothing one can do. This position robs one of personal power. Conversely, people from these historically oppressed groups who understand oppression are able to confront dysfunctional systems and network with others to take control of their personal and professional lives. They are not seduced by tokenism but work with their colleagues to become leaders in developing policies and practices that serve the historically underserved.

Personal Responsibility. The challenge for many of us who confront the concept of entitlement for the first time is that the benefits are often unrecognized and unacknowledged. The privileges of entitlement—to the entitled—are often invisible and appear to be just the way the world is. Entitled people may see oppression, be disgusted by it, and never consider that they have directly benefited from the systematic oppression of others. To become aware of and to acknowledge entitlement is a sign of growth and strength. To understand both oppression and entitlement is the first step to self-determination and personal responsibility.

Figure 3.4 presents oppression and entitlement as being similarly dysfunctional. The functional alternatives are self-determination and personal responsibility.

Figure 3.4 Functional and Dysfunctional Reactions to Oppression and Entitlement

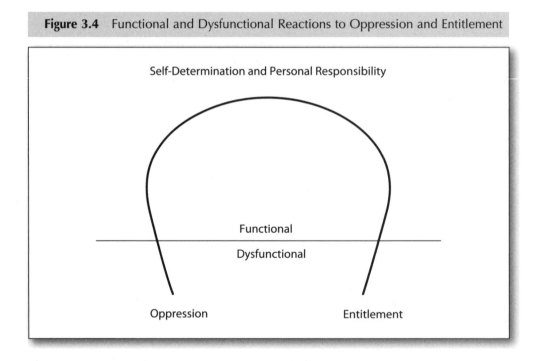

After entitled people understand and recognize oppression and the benefits of entitlement, they then have a moral choice to make. To do nothing, once informed, is tantamount to the immoral position of conspirator. The moral position is to commit oneself to end oppression. Although entitled people may work with oppressed groups to oppose acts of oppression, their major responsibility is to work within schools and districts to raise the consciousness of the uninformed entitled. They focus their energies on changing policies, practices, and behaviors that perpetuate oppression and entitlement, recognizing that the two are inextricably interconnected.

Similar to the discussion about movement from anger and guilt to confidence, educators who transcend the oppression and entitlement responses and, instead, opt for self-determination and personal responsibility have demonstrated the willingness to reflect on their practices for the purpose of providing their students access to high-quality educational experiences. Educators such as these demonstrate the ability to reflect on their practices while working with students, as well as to think back on their practices, for the purpose of continuous improvement. These educators have made the shift in thinking from cultural destructiveness, cultural incapacity, and cultural blindness to cultural precompetence and cultural competence. The language of these educators shifts from "why these students cannot succeed" to statements such as "These are different ways in which I would like to approach my work with our students."

Informed, entitled people understand that to confront unacknowledged privileges inherent in institutional values, policies, and practices that perpetuate disparity takes keen insight and commitment to moral authority. School leaders can be pivotal in ensuring that we, all of us, are part of the discussions about diversity. Let us revisit Joan and Connie, who have been talking about these issues, and see how they are handling these topics:

Joan:	Okay, so I am beginning to understand. My feelings are more about resistance than anything. I can see that now. I can't say that I am totally comfortable with this whole notion yet, but I can appreciate that we have to do something. I am beginning to understand your feedback that I want to "short-circuit" the system of learning about Cultural Proficiency.
Connie:	With that, we can make a start. How is it you recognize, within yourself, that you have been avoiding the deeper learning?
Joan:	Well, it has to do with the presentation the other day. I have been thinking—no, hoping—that all of this fuss about diversity was that I was going to need to learn particular strategies in working with low-performing students.
Connie:	How do you see it now?
Joan:	I am not totally certain, but I know it has to involve my looking at what I expect from my students, how I interact with them, and my knowledge of how students learn. In some ways, it is as if I am starting all over again as a teacher.
Connie:	Yes, it is about learning and unlearning; however, the main difference between now and when we began our roles as educators is that we have a storehouse of knowledge of what does and what does not work.

Joan:	Well, this diversity training must be awfully burdensome for you.
Connie:	How do you mean?
Joan:	You already know all of this stuff, don't you?
Connie:	Hardly! Though I am a person of color, there is much for me to learn about working with all groups. However, probably the most important role I see for myself is to make sure that I keep these issues on the table for all of us to face. That is a challenge that I welcome.
Joan:	Yeah. And, that is a challenge I have to share with you. It is like the speaker said the other day: "We have to approach each of these students like we would want people to approach our own children." That sure makes it personal.

Being culturally precompetent is often described as knowing what you do not know. It is not having the answers but being able to know when current practices are not serving students. Cultural precompetent educators demonstrate a willingness to learn about their students' cultures, learning styles, and communities in which they live. Culturally competent educators reflect on their practices using the lens of the five Essential Elements—assessing their cultural knowledge, valuing diversity, managing the dynamics of difference, adapting to diversity, and institutionalizing cultural knowledge. Culturally competent educators are committed to the inside-out approach of Cultural Proficiency as they continuously examine their values and behaviors and seek to improve their practices.

Reflective Activity

In Chapter 6, we will invite you to identify three bold steps for Cultural Proficiency at your school. How might this chapter inform that process for you?

_____

_____

_____

_____

What questions do you have to guide your continued learning?

_____

_____

Dr. Brewer left that day confident the Maple View Elementary School had begun the task of moving forward with learning how to move the staff and the school toward being culturally proficient. He sat in his car for a few minutes to reflect on today's session. He thought to himself,

I think the leaders at this school are beginning to view reform as a very personal, transformative choice. I do know that learning about entitlement and privilege will be a continuous challenge for all of us. However, we have to continuously ask ourselves, "In what ways can I change my practices to benefit all students?"

Chapter 4 presents the Guiding Principles of Cultural Proficiency as core values for your consideration. The Guiding Principles provide a healthy, constructive path for developing personal and organizational effectiveness in widening the purpose of schools in ways that serve all students equitably.

4 Cultural Proficiency in Practice

The Guiding Principles

Leaders mobilize people to face problems, and communities make progress on problems because leaders challenge and help them to do so.

—Ronald Heifetz (1994, pp. 14–15)

SAM BREWER: THE MAKING OF A CULTURALLY PROFICIENT LEADER

During the 25 years that Dr. Sam Brewer has been professionally involved in public education, he has become increasingly more aware of the cultural obstacles students face in schools and classrooms and the effects those obstacles have on student access, learning, and achievement. As a white male and high school principal, he was startled when first learning what he didn't know about issues of systemic oppression.

Sam was amazed at how naïve he had been in the early part of his career. Though he recognized concepts such as racism, sexism, and classism, he actually thought them more historical than current reality. However, two events changed his perspectives, and his life, in ways he could not have predicted. When he first was asked by a district office administrator to consider becoming an assistant principal, he was honored but conflicted. He loved being a classroom teacher and was highly regarded by peers, students, and parents as a stellar teacher committed to all students being successful. His mentor made a persuasive point that as an administrator, he could do even more to positively impact students' lives. Additionally, the course of study at Maple View State University with its social justice focus served to reinforce his mentor's suggestion of the potential extent of his influence as a formal school leader. Second, Dr. Campbell, the former superintendent, appointed him to the district's initial Cultural Proficiency Task Force. Though he was not knowledgeable about Cultural Proficiency, he trusted that she saw in him the potential for cross-cultural effectiveness. After years of experience as an assistant principal and, then, as principal, he had learned that the "-isms" in their many forms could be combated by educators making deep personal commitments to democratize their practice. Today, he realized that Dr. Campbell and his other mentors had groomed him for this day.

Taking a few last sips of coffee at the small, round table in his kitchen, Sam reviews his notes for the principals' meeting later this morning. It would be so simple if he could just mandate Cultural Proficiency in every school. He sits back in his chair and smiles slightly, knowing that such a mandate is impossible. He also knows that people will look at his behavior as an example of the changes he wants them to make in their own behavior. He has thought about this meeting for so long—and now, in just a few hours, he will be sitting with these former colleague principals and preparing them to embark on a journey toward cultural competence with the teachers in their schools. Glancing at the clock, he sees it is time to go.

Later, in the conference room, Dr. Brewer asks the principals to reflect on a simple but important question: "Whose needs does your school best serve?" "Students," says Talma Moore-Stuart, the recently appointed principal of Pine Hills High School. Sam smiles and responds enthusiastically, "Great!" He then asks Talma and the other principals to consider which group or groups of students are most successful and why:

> I don't want an answer right now. I want you to meet with your school's leadership team and review your students' achievement results. Look at every demographic group and determine who is doing well and who is not succeeding. And then ask yourselves two questions: "Why are we getting these results?" and "Are these the results we want?"

Standing up, Sam distributes each school's achievement reports. Pointing out that the results are disaggregated by student demographic groups, Sam says,

> It's very important to understand the dynamics in your schools that are producing the results you're getting. Go back and study these results with your teams. Then study your schools. What are your expectations for each demographic group? Are you meeting those expectations? Why?

Sitting down again, Sam lowers his voice, saying,

When we meet again in two weeks, I want each of you to be prepared to describe the obstacles that seem to be getting in the way of student achievement for each demographic group. I also want you to be ready to discuss how the norms for expected behavior, the structures—like scheduling and grouping, the patterns of activity, and the rules and procedures in the school—may be contributing to the obstacles your students are experiencing.

Sam hands each principal a set of data collection sheets and tells them,

This packet will guide your work with your teams. You'll see that I'm asking you to think about the dynamics of your schools in relation to the Principles of Cultural Proficiency that support our district mission. Oh, and one other very important thing, I want you to work with your teams to identify five strong values that make your school the school it is.

Sam stands up and concludes,

I'll see you in two weeks. Call me if any questions come up. I'm looking forward to our next meeting. And thanks for being on time today. It shows respect for everyone's time and for our time together as a group. I really appreciate that.

Reflective Activity

Consider the questions that the superintendent, Dr. Brewer, asked the principals in his district: Which groups of students are best served by your school? Which students are not well served? Why are you getting these results?

- As you reflect on your own district, school, classroom, or program, how would you respond to these important questions?
- How is your own leadership informed by your response?

_____

_____

_____

_____

MOBILIZING COMMUNITIES TO MAKE PROGRESS— WITHOUT EASY ANSWERS

A culturally proficient leader influences others to make changes in their values, beliefs, and attitudes in ways that are inclusive of all cultural groups of students. Challenging and supporting others to build their capacity to confront difficult sociocultural problems in their community and to take them on successfully is a priority for a leader intent on fostering culturally proficient behavior among others. Indeed, such a leader makes it his or her purpose to help the community become culturally proficient and support in building productive, functional patterns of social interaction.

In our work with schools and districts, we find that vision, mission, and core value statements often satisfy some external accreditation requirements rather than guide or give purpose to the real work of the school or district. As an alternative to such practice, leaders can choose to offer authentic benchmarks of progress by charting a course when considering core values informed by the Guiding Principles of Cultural Proficiency. To use them effectively in this way requires understanding the Guiding Principles at a deep level and embracing them as core leadership values. The Guiding Principles are as follows:

- Culture is a predominant force in people's and school's lives.
- The dominant culture serves people in varying degrees.
- People have both personal identities and group identities.
- Diversity within cultures is vast and significant.
- Each individual and each group has unique cultural values and needs.
- The best of both worlds enhances the capacity of all.
- The family, as defined by each culture, is the primary system of support in the education of children.
- School systems must recognize that marginalized populations have to be at least bicultural and that this status creates a unique set of issues to which the system must be equipped to respond.
- Inherent in cross-cultural interaction are dynamics that must be acknowledged, adjusted to, and accepted.

THE GUIDING PRINCIPLES OF CULTURALLY PROFICIENT LEADERSHIP

More often than not, when educators talk about school change, they describe modifications in the structures, patterns, and processes of education practice. Structural changes such as adopting new scheduling patterns or new grouping procedures, or even requiring new curriculum materials, do have the potential to reform instructional practices and thereby improve student learning for some students. However, structural changes alone are insufficient to produce the kinds of deep conversions that have the potential to transform the social and cultural conditions within a school or district.

The Guiding Principles of Cultural Proficiency offer a pathway for school leaders to shift their perspectives on school change from reforming structures, policies, and rules in schools to transforming relationships, interactions, and behaviors of the people within schools. Holders of the school reform perspective concentrate their efforts on how to change structures and policies. The school reform perspective too often flows from a predictable mission statement that espouses goals that are not reflective of the authentic day-to-day practices of people in the school. A commonplace mission statement purports that all students can achieve at a high level; however, in practice this espoused goal ignores the fact that many students from identifiable demographic groups do not succeed. In not having an authentic mission statement, schools with a reform perspective resort to default mission statements with an implicit core belief that some children and youth cannot or will not learn. Reeves (2000) notes that this unstated belief is expressed in code words, such as "diversity" and "demographics." In a school with a reform perspective, one might hear, "We're not doing too badly, given our diversity" (or demographics).

Conversely, the school leader who holds a transformative perspective, recognizing that achievement inequities mirror the larger societal inequities, focuses on leadership and school practices to meet the capabilities, opportunities, and needs of diverse communities. Leaders engaged in transformative activities use their knowledge of the larger community to build on the experiences of their students. They direct their own leadership activities in ways that involve all members of the school or district community in becoming culturally proficient and prepared to meet the challenging problems they encounter together.

Dr. Brewer believes the Guiding Principles open up opportunities to build culturally proficient and functionally diverse schools and school districts in which people interact with one another in respectful and culturally responsive ways. From a recent issue of his state leadership journal, he posted a series of questions for the leadership team to consider. The questions were designed to promote reflection and dialogue to support the Guiding Principles as core values for Maple View schools:

- To what extent do you honor culture as a natural and normal part of the community you serve?
- To what extent do you recognize and understand the differential and historical treatment accorded to those least well served in our schools?

- When working with a person whose culture is different from yours, to what extent do you see the person as both an individual and as a member of a cultural group?
- To what extent do you recognize and value the differences within the cultural communities you serve?
- To what extent do you know and respect the unique needs of cultural groups in the community you serve?
- To what extent do you know how cultural groups in your community define family and the manner in which family serves as the primary system of support for students?
- To what extent do you recognize and understand the bicultural reality for cultural groups historically not well served in our schools?
- To what extent do you recognize your role in acknowledging, adjusting to, and accepting cross-cultural interactions as necessary social and communications dynamics?
- To what extent do you incorporate cultural knowledge into educational practices and policy-making? (Lindsey, Terrell, Nuri Robins, & Lindsey, 2010, pp. 12–15)

There was nodding, a few quizzical looks, and side conversations among members as they examined the reflective questions. A few members acknowledged having seen the article, but only two or three had read it. When he sensed a mood of curiosity, Dr. Brewer proceeded by saying, "Two weeks ago we began to consider school values that support all students learning. Let's take a few moments and read an excerpt from the article that is the source for the questions I posted on the whiteboard. Then we'll engage in a conversation." Members took their copies of the article, moved to comfortable locations in the room, and began to read.

FOCUS ON ASSETS, OVERCOME BARRIERS

School leaders can shift the culture from responding to learning gaps as compliance issues and responding in ways that transform organization.

Inclusive approach to closing learning gaps

Are our school districts leaving out the role of district office leaders and boards of education as important links to closing the achievement gap? Since the recent "discovery" of the achievement gap (the theme for this issue of *Leadership* more appropriately has identified it as "learning gap"), we in the education community have placed more attention on assessment and accountability than at any time in our history. Much of the impetus for this attention has been as the result of sanctions built within California's Public Schools Accountability Act (1999) and No Child Left Behind (2002).

A barrier to closing the learning gaps in many of our schools is one over which we have direct influence, namely resistance to change. Systemic reform, or change, has become an important phrase for school leaders to use in addressing learning needs/gaps vertically throughout our school systems, from the superintendent and board of education to the classroom.

However, the usual attention for change focuses on teachers and site administrators (principals and assistant principals). When the focus is on changing the behavior of only those at the school site, systemic change is ignored.

Surfacing values, beliefs, and assumptions

We invite you to read the following nine questions and the brief discussions that follow and employ your skills of reflection and dialogue. First, read each question and the comments and reflect on your personal responses. Ask yourself, "What is my truthful, honest response to each question and how do I react to the comments that follow each question?"

Educational leaders who are willing to look deep within themselves to examine the *why* of *how* they developed certain attitudes and values are well prepared to lead schools serving diverse communities.

Second, in your role as school leader—county, district, or site level—we invite you to engage with your colleagues in dialogue to surface deeply held assumptions and reach shared understanding of what "closing the learning gap" means to the school community. From these inclusive dialogue sessions carefully crafted statements will emerge to inform everyone in your school community of your shared beliefs and values about all students learning.

These nine questions are designed as guides for individual educators and school districts to probe and understand their core values in working with communities that have populations with cultural characteristics different from their own.

The purpose of these questions and comments is to actualize the intent of this quote, often attributed to Malcolm X: "Don't tell me what you value, tell me what you do and I will tell you what you value."

Nine Questions for Reflection and Dialogue

1. **To what extent do you honor culture as a natural and normal part of the community you serve?**

   The Public Schools Accountability Act and No Child Left Behind have brought us face-to-face with the reality of cultural demographic groups in ways that we have never before experienced in this country. Though always present, we now have the opportunity to discuss student learning in terms of race, ethnicity, gender, ableness, and language learning.

(Continued)

(Continued)

Each educator and each school district must recognize the extent to which we regard these and other cultural groupings as asset-rich resources upon which to build our educational programs, not as accountability inconveniences, deficits, or sources of problems.

2. **To what extent do you recognize and understand the differential and historical treatment accorded to those least well served in our schools?**

The disparities that we have come to acknowledge as the achievement or learning gap in many cases have been developed over many generations. Though we may not have been party to intentional practices of segregation, racism, sexism, ethnocentrism, or any other form of oppression, it is our collective responsibility to recognize the historical and current bases of discrimination and assume responsibility for rectifying and correcting past injustices through socially just actions now.

Initiating socially just actions begins with recognizing how many of us today have privileges earned by being members of dominant groups. Responsibility for change must begin with those of us in the education community and the manner in which we see the achievement/learning gap as *our* issue.

3. **When working with a person whose culture is different from yours, to what extent do you see the person as both an individual and as a member of a cultural group?**

We estimate that all of us like to be seen and valued for who we are. We may enjoy being part of a team that achieves; however, one's group identity does not detract from also wanting to be appreciated for who we are as individuals. Yet, when working in cross-cultural venues, some educators too often revert to use of terms such as *they* and *them* when referencing people from cultural groups different from themselves. At best, this often gives rise to the "model minority syndrome" that occurs when one member of the dominated group learns the cultural norms of the dominant group. At worst, this leads to pitting one cultural group against another and asks, "Why can't you be like (the other group)?" or other forms of scapegoating.

4. **To what extent do you recognize and value the differences within the cultural communities you serve?**

The cultural groups in our schools are no more monoliths than those of us educators who populate the ranks within our schools. Each of the cultural groups we serve has vast differences in education, incomes, faith practices, and lifestyles. The cultural groups in our school communities are as diverse as is the broader community. The socioeconomic differences within cultural groups often give rise to groups having more similar worldviews across socioeconomic lines than they do within cultural groups.

5. **To what extent do you know and respect the unique needs of cultural groups in the community you serve?**

A one-size-fits-all approach to education may serve the needs of school at the expense of our students and their communities. Even within schools that have all students conform to grooming standards and physical accommodations, educators have learned to acknowledge in their curriculum and in their teaching different learning styles, different cognitive styles, and the different ways people process information.

The inclusive educator teaches and encourages colleagues to make the necessary adaptations in how schools provide educational service so that all people have access to the same benefits and privileges as members of the dominant group in society.

6. **To what extent do you know how cultural groups in your community define family and the manner in which family serves as the primary system of support for students?**

Prevalent educational practice has been to assume that parents and other family caregivers who really care about the education of their children will avail themselves of opportunities to interact with the school. Increasingly, our schools have become adept at finding culturally inclusive ways of engaging parents and caregivers in support of student achievement.

We find too often educators and parents have different perceptions of the term "parent participation." Lawson used the terms "community centric" and "school centric" to describe these contrasting perceptions.

- *Community centric.* "Parents involved in activities that meet the basic needs of their children as going to school well fed, rested and clean."

- *School centric.* "Parents involved in activities that are structured and defined for parents by schools" (Lawson as cited in Lindsey, Nuri Robins, & Terrell, 2009, p. 150). Effective and meaningful partnerships between parents and schools require sensitive, respectful, and caring school leaders willing to learn the positive nature and culture of the community and to identify barriers that have impeded progress in school-community relations. Tahoe Elementary School in Sacramento and San Marcos Elementary School have identified their core values about parent/ guardian involvement and have been successful in engaging parents in productive ways through school-site, home, and other off-site meetings.

The traditional, often stereotypic, image of Euro-American homes of family identified as one mother, one father, and the children is now recognized as a limited view of "family." Today, culturally proficient school leaders acknowledge single-parent families, multiple-generation extended families, same-gender parents, foster care homes, and residential care homes as "family." Whatever the configuration for the children in our schools, their family is their family.

7. **To what extent do you recognize and understand the bicultural reality for cultural groups historically not well served in our schools?**

Parents/guardians and their children have to be fluent in the communication patterns of the school as well as the communication patterns that exist in their

(Continued)

(Continued)

communities. They also have to know the cultural norms and expectations of schools, which may conflict or be different from those in their communities, their countries of origin or their cultural groups.

In ideal conditions, their children are developing bicultural skills, learning to "code switch" to meet the cultural expectations of their environments. However, parents may not have these skills for adapting to new and different environments. Parents or guardians and their children are then penalized because they do not respond to the norms set by educators because they do not navigate well the educational systems of the public schools.

8. **To what extent do you recognize your role in acknowledging, adjusting to, and accepting cross-cultural interactions as necessary social and communications dynamics?**

We have encountered few educators who fail to recognize the historical and current impact of racism and other forms of oppression on current school environments. It is also our experience that our educator colleagues who do recognize and understand the huge toll that oppression takes also understand how people not affected by those same systems benefit in unwitting ways. It is precisely the awareness of the dynamic nature of oppression versus entitlement that enables such educators to be effective in responding to the educational needs of cultural groups within their schools and districts.

Unless one has experienced intentional or unintentional acts of discrimination or oppression, a person cannot fathom the everyday toll it takes on one's day-to-day life experiences. The overrepresentation of students of color in special education programs and their underrepresentation in advanced placement and gifted and talented programs is not new information. Educators who are aware of such dynamics employ strategies and tactics that engage parents as partners in beneficial placements for their children.

9. **To what extent do you incorporate cultural knowledge into educational practices and policy-making?**

Experienced educational leaders recognize the need to learn the culture of a new organization. Their very survival depends on appropriate responses to cultural norms of the school community. Effective educational leaders are aware of their own cultures and their impact on their school or district.

Knowledge about school culture, our individual cultures, and the cultures of our community rarely arrives to our desktops in a three-ring notebook or a PDF file. Cultural knowledge is possessed by those who are keenly aware of themselves, their community surroundings, and the legacies and challenges experienced by cultural groups in our country and local communities.

Educational leaders who possess this self awareness are effective in cross-cultural settings and avoid phrases such as, "Doesn't everyone know that?" "I would hope parents see that as their responsibility," or "It's the way we do things here and they will have to adjust." Phrases such as these marginalize outsiders and serve to perpetuate an "us against them" mentality.

Culturally proficient leaders share their own cultural knowledge, engage with the community, and invite community experts, knowing that such actions over time will lead to appropriately institutionalizing cultural knowledge. Such leaders recognize that re-culturing schools to be responsive to diverse constituencies is an internal and intentional process.

Responses to these nine questions can be the basis for Guiding Principles, or core values, that inform and support culturally proficient leadership. The principles help frame and focus the behaviors of teachers and school leaders intentionally on all students learning at levels higher than ever reached before.

Use internal assets and be intentional

The learning gaps are ours to rectify. Shifting the culture of a school district from responding to learning gaps as compliance issues to responding in ways that transform organizational culture relies on use of school leaders' internal assets of reflection and dialogue. This intentionality is a two-step process of personal reflection and purposeful dialogue with colleagues.

Responses to these nine questions also provide the basis for developing mission statements and core values intended to serve a diverse community. To be effective in schools today leaders need strong core personal and organizational values (Collins & Porras, 1997; Lindsey, Jungwirth, Pahl, & Lindsey, 2009; Senge, 2000).

In addition to the values you currently hold, the values of Cultural Proficiency explicit in the nine Guiding Principles can serve as the foundation on which to re-culture and transform schools and districts.

Once members completed reading the article, they were afforded a few minutes to record thoughts and feelings and to pose questions to guide their own professional learning as well as questions to guide their work in their schools. Near the close of the session, Dr. Brewer led a thoughtful conversation about how other people might recognize our values when they visit our schools. The principals resonated with the line from the article, "Don't tell me what you value, tell me what you do and I will tell you what you value." What might have been a defensive analysis of school and district mission, vision, and core value statements a few months ago was now thoughtful comments on how to manage change that focuses on students and their cultures as assets.

Dr. Brewer noted that the next two monthly meetings were to be devoted to Common Core State Standards topics and that the lens of

Cultural Proficiency would be a useful perspective during those sessions. He continued by noting that since the next Cultural Proficiency session was scheduled three months away, he would like for everyone to return to their schools and to listen and look for evidence of Barriers to Cultural Proficiency as well as expressions of core values consistent with the Guiding Principles discussed today. Members nodded in assent and asked, "What should we return with?" Dr. Brewer responded, "Let's return with our stories. That should give us a strong sense of where we are as a district. From that point, we can become increasingly intentional in our Cultural Proficiency journey."

CORE VALUE EXPRESSIONS IN MAPLE VIEW SCHOOL DISTRICT

In the brief situations that follow, we return to Maple View School District to examine the dynamics of culture at work in schools. Each situation represents a composite of actual events and authentic conversations that we have observed during our work with PK–12 schools across the United States and Canada. Keep in mind that these are conversations of educators engaged in the challenging work of personal transformation.

The conversations address educational issues related to the ways in which educators recognize and respond to their students. When educators hold a view of a student sharing characteristics of a cultural group that they do not share with others outside the group, while also viewing the student as an individual with an idiosyncratic expression of those cultural characteristics, they position themselves to deal with both the individual and the culture. How educators respond to students from culturally diverse populations influences what students learn and how they learn it. Teachers should be well prepared to instruct students in various content areas, and they must be sensitive to the ways in which a student's culture impacts what and how he or she learns. The first story is from Pine Hills High School and relates to the faculty's decision to acknowledge the group identities of gay and lesbian students.

Conversation: Pine Hills High School and Harassment

The leadership committee at Pine Hills High School has become increasingly aware of an emerging issue rising from gay and lesbian students sharing their sexual orientation identities in classroom discussions and during cocurricular club meetings. For most of the students at the school, this topic is a relative nonissue; however, a small group of male students has begun to harass the gay and lesbian students. Last week, a gay student was beaten severely after a football game. Talma Moore-Stuart, the principal at Pine Hills, convened the leadership committee on Monday afternoon following the assault. The following conversation took place at the meeting:

Talma Moore-Stuart:	We simply can't tolerate this kind of behavior on this campus. It's up to us around this table to make sure this violence stops!
Jim Jones (P.E. Teacher; Coach)	I couldn't agree more. Maybe we need to get these students some counseling to help them with their sexual preference or choice, or whatever their problem is.
Alice Falls (History Teacher):	Jim. The term is sexual orientation. Your orientation is to heterosexuality. The students who are the targets in this assault were attacked because they have a homosexual orientation. I know that some folks try to make this a moral issue or a mental health issue. You suggested these students need counseling.
Jim:	Well, I wanted to get them some help. They have been threatened and hurt. Some counseling might help.
Alice:	Counseling in order to become "normal"? Their problem isn't that they are not normal; they have a different sexual orientation from their abusers. They are different from you and me, that's all. What they need most is fairness from all of us.
Talma:	Intolerance and misunderstanding historically have been used against any group that is "different" from mainstream, from what the majority or dominant group thinks is acceptable or normal.
Jim:	I am beginning to see what you guys are saying.
Alice:	Look at our history. Women couldn't vote or own property or do certain jobs because they weren't men. Black folks couldn't be free, couldn't vote because they weren't white. The dominant group uses its power to say what's okay and what's not okay.
Talma:	For us, right now, right here at Pine Hills High School, the issue is that we are responsible for educating all of our students well. If we are going to teach our gay and lesbian students effectively, we

must acknowledge them for who they are. We also must remember that in addition to being gay or lesbian, they are still individual Pine Hills students— math students, history students, athletes, student leaders, and the children of folks in this community.

Jim: You know, I hope I don't come across as thoughtless, but you guys are raising things I have never even thought about. I mean, I guess I knew this stuff at some level, but I feel like I'm on information overload. You know, right now I just need to think about this. You've opened my eyes; thanks for helping me see this. Man, I feel really awkward.

Jim is shifting his perspective as a result of a conversation with his colleagues. What was it about the conversation that helped him become more aware of his assumptions?

Reflective and Dialogic Activity

Which Guiding Principles are involved in this story? Consider the way this conversation influenced Jim and helped him to rethink his assumptions about a group of students. Now that his awareness of this issue is heightened, how can Jim learn to recognize and acknowledge the identity of gay and lesbian students while accepting and respecting them as individuals? In what ways does Jim's learning apply to other cultural groups of students?

Conversation: Maple View Elementary School Has Culture

Laura Alvarez is beginning her second year as the assistant principal of Maple View Elementary School. This year, she and her staff have made a commitment to increase their students' math and reading literacy. Working with the district's math and language arts specialists, Laura has helped her staff recognize some of the unique educational needs of the diverse populations among their students. Maple View Elementary has three distinct demographic groups: newly arrived immigrants from Mexico who are primarily English language learners, second-generation Mexican American students whose families are struggling financially, and African American students who live in public housing and whose families are also struggling financially. Laura and the teachers at Maple View understand that each subgroup of students has specific learning needs and will benefit from instructional strategies that are designed to build on their individual strengths while responding to their specific needs as a group. Laura also knows that each of her grade-level teams has its own culture and particular way of interacting with one another. Listen to her conversation with the district's math specialist, Dr. Belinda Jackson, as they plan a professional development program for the year:

Belinda:	Laura, I'm so excited about this new math adoption program, and I'm really interested to know how you are planning to help the staff with implementation.
Laura:	Well, thanks to you, the district is providing us with two professional development days in August for the publishing company representatives to begin the training. We have all the materials on campus already, so I'm thinking that their training will be just a general orientation. While all of this is good, I'm feeling uneasy and I'm not sure why.
Belinda:	Okay, Laura, talk to me about "being uneasy." What's that all about?
Laura:	Oh, Belinda, it's just that, well, candidly, some of our teams are ready to go and others are not.
Belinda:	It's just like one of your favorite phrases, "We're talking about the elephant in the middle of the room that no one can see."
Laura:	Belinda, what are you talking about? What does that mean?
Belinda:	Laura, we've talked about this before. You've told me that it's no secret; each grade-level team has its own culture.
Laura:	You're absolutely right, Belinda! It doesn't matter what I give the second-grade team, they're going to take it and run with it. At the other end of the continuum is the fifth-grade team. They can hardly stand to be in the same room at the same time. Developing collaborative relationships among them is going to take a very specific strategy.
Belinda:	So, okay, now we know what we've got to do. Let's get to work.
Laura (sighing):	Yes, we sure do! Coaching is going to be different from team to team. Thanks, Belinda! You're always such a great help to me. What would I do without you?

Laura and Belinda have acknowledged the different cultures that exist among the grade-level teams, and now they are better prepared to meet the needs of students through meeting the diverse needs of each team.

Reflective and Dialogic Activity

Which Guiding Principles are involved in this story? Consider the way this conversation influenced Laura and helped give her the direction she needed to meet the differing professional development needs of her grade-level groups. Now that she recognizes the differences and understands why they exist, how should she move forward with her planning?

_____

_____

_____

_____

The next conversation provides us with insight as to how differences within racial or ethnic cultural groups might be manifested.

Conversation: Maple View Arts Magnet School and Stereotyping

The Maple View Arts Magnet School is a small district kindergarten through Grade 8 (K–8) charter school supported by a group of parents who want to develop educational opportunities in the visual and performing arts for their own and other children in the district. The mission of the school is to foster each student's individual talents in the arts and to support his or her overall academic success. Students who graduate from the K–8 program are able to go directly into the district's arts magnet high school.

Ella Chapman is an African American parent of two students enrolled in Maple View Arts. Her son, Jeffrey, is a seventh grader, and her daughter, Cheryl, is in the fourth grade. Both children are musically gifted and often perform with the local musical theater group. Ella and her husband, Gregory, are also talented professional musicians who met while they were students at the Juilliard School of Music in New York City. They both perform professionally in the regional symphony orchestra.

Anh Me Vu is a Vietnamese parent whose daughter, Melanie, is a member of the school's corps de ballet. Melanie Vu is in the sixth grade, and her brother Jason is a third grader. Melanie is an accomplished musician and a talented dancer. Jason is showing skill as a young violinist. Anh Me, a gifted musician herself, also attended Juilliard and performs regularly with the regional symphony orchestra.

Let's listen to this conversation between the two parents following a recital at the school:

Ella (smiling warmly):	Anh Me, it's so good to see you. Your Melanie is such a beautiful dancer. Is she considering joining a professional ballet company's school?

Anh Me:	Oh, Ella, it's good to see you, too. Our rehearsals last week with the symphony were pretty grueling, weren't they? I've been recovering over the weekend.
Ella:	That was quite a workout all right.
Anh Me:	Ella, thanks for the generous praise for Melanie. She works very hard at developing her dancing, and she loves it. I'm not sure she's ready to commit to it as a career. We'll just have to wait and see. And, Ella, you must be very proud of Jeffrey. I understand that he placed first in the regional violin competition last week. I hope our son, Jason, will someday play as well as your son Jeffrey does.
Ella:	Yes, we are very proud of Jeffrey. Musical talent seems to run in our family. Our family, like yours, has had three generations attend Julliard. Jeffrey will be the fourth generation.
Anh Me:	Wow, I am surprised you knew I attended Julliard, too! Most people look at me and my family and think we just arrived from Viet Nam and can't speak English.
Ella:	I do understand that frustration, believe me. I've lived with it my entire life.
Anh Me:	You know, when Melanie first applied to attend the arts magnet, one of the panelists asked her if her family was one of the "boat people." Melanie didn't know what the woman was talking about. That didn't stop this woman; she went on and said she was surprised Melanie spoke English so clearly. Melanie didn't know what to make of it, and I was totally exasperated. I went up to her after the interview and told her that in addition to English, every member of our family is fluent in Vietnamese and French! I'm not sure I had any impact on her stereotypes, I'm afraid that's just the way she sees the world.
Ella:	Listen, Anh Me, I can relate to that! You did the right thing in calling her on her stereotyping. I know it's sometimes hard to do, but we can't just accept that kind of thoughtlessness. I'll admit that it's happening less and less often, but our family sometimes still experiences the same kind of insensitivity. It gets so old, but we've got to stay on top of it and educate others when it happens.

This conversation illustrates the experiences of two individuals stunned by thoughtless, insensitive stereotyping. The cultural group that individuals are part of may be organizational, economic, educational, racial, or occupational. Regardless, there is always tremendous individual diversity and variation within the group. Individual differences among the members of a group are as important to the development of a person's self-image and identity as is membership within that group. Educators have the unique opportunity to continue to learn about the members of the communities they serve, both as members of their cultural communities and as the individuals they are.

Reflective and Dialogic Activity

Which Guiding Principles are involved in this story? Consider the way this conversation helped the two parents, Ella and Anh Me, understand and appreciate more fully each other's unique characteristics and background. How can they put this new learning to use in countering and diminishing thoughtless and insensitive stereotyping of themselves and their families and also other unique members of their cultural groups?

_____

_____

_____

_____

Conversation: Maple View School District Leadership 'Hears'

Dr. Sam Brewer, the superintendent of the Maple View School District, and his administrative team are taking seriously their commitment to develop an organizational culture and behavior expectations that are consistent with the Guiding Principles of culturally proficient practice. The principals have interviewed colleagues at their schools in an effort to comply with Dr. Brewer's assignment to describe obstacles to student achievement for each subgroup of students at their schools. These interview data are one of the indicators they will use to guide their planning.

A group of the white administrators were interested to see what, if any, stereotypes they would glean from their colleagues at their schools. Let's listen to the conversation that is emerging as the second day in the series begins with Dr. Andrew, their facilitator:

Andy:	Well, as I look across the room at data arrayed on your tables, it is clear you have collected a lot of data.
Tony:	You're right about that, Andy. This was an interesting assignment. I learned a lot by asking my teachers the questions.
Fred (laughing):	Well, Tony, don't keep us in suspense, what are your findings?
Tony:	I learned some pretty interesting things, but right now I am more interested to know why Hector has that astonished look on his face.

Hector:	I don't know if you're seeing astonishment or feelings of foolishness!
Andy:	Wow, that sounds pretty heavy! What's going on?
Hector:	Well, I am feeling stupid. That's what's going on.
Fred:	Hector, we're all here to learn. The only stupidity would be closing ourselves off from looking at the data and learning from it.
Hector:	Well, this is kind of embarrassing. At Pine Hills High School, we use a pretty derogatory name to identify a group of kids who come from that area across the highway where there's a lot of unemployment and people are struggling financially.
Andy:	This is showing up in the data you collected?
Hector:	Yeah, I think that's why it hit me so hard. We refer to those kids as "the trailer park kids." Looking at my data spread our here in front of me, I see that we use this label to pigeonhole and stereotype those kids. I can't believe I didn't see this before now.
Fred:	That's why looking at this kind of real data is so important. It helps us see patterns of behavior that we just take for granted or overlook because it's "just what we do." It's that kind of unconscious stereotyping and the assumption behind the stereotyping that are so harmful. We stereotype the group and treat them as a solid block rather than a group of unique individuals.
Andy:	Hector, your recognizing that stereotyping pattern in your data has helped all of us learn something very important—stereotypes and their embedded assumptions can't be changed if we can't, or don't, see them.

This conversation reveals how assumptions about a cultural group such as the "trailer park kids" can transcend traditionally identified cultural groups and still stereotype all members of a group and keep them locked out of the opportunity to be academically and socially successful individuals. The assumptions and stereotypes that educators have about the potential of a group and its capacity to be successful can cause them to react to all members of the group with generalized low expectations rather than responding to the unique individual potential and educational needs of each group member. Culturally proficient educational leaders must be vigilant in recognizing the deleterious impact of insensitive, thoughtless stereotyping of students and, moreover, must intervene with equal vigilance to ensure students an educational environment that is not culturally or socially detrimental to their individual success as learners.

Reflective and Dialogic Activity

Which Guiding Principles are involved in this story? Think about your own assumptions and stereotypes about people from cultures other than yours or about students whose living situations may be much different from yours. How do assumptions and stereotypes block you from responding thoughtfully and respectfully toward others?

APPLYING GUIDING PRINCIPLES TO YOUR PRACTICE

Now, put your knowledge to use. During the next several days, do as the Maple View Leadership Team did and listen for how people in your school or office address issues of culture. Note levels of comfort with conversation about culture and diversity. Observe how people describe their colleagues, students, and members of the community who are culturally different from them. Pay attention to how they describe people who speak languages other than English. Monitor how you describe those who are culturally different from you. The adjectives you and your colleagues use will give you insight to each of your values in this area. After a few days, ask yourself: "What am I learning about my colleagues and about me? In what ways do the Guiding Principles guide us in identifying obstacles to student achievement?"

With this chapter, you have covered two of the Tools of Cultural Proficiency, Barriers and Guiding Principles. You have a good sense of personal institutional barriers to student success in our schools and knowledge of the Guiding Principles of Cultural Proficiency as core values that, when held as core beliefs, are aides on your Cultural Proficiency journey. Chapter 5 presents the Continuum. The Continuum is a tool that allows you to identify values, behaviors, policies, and practices that are informed by the Barriers and differentiate them from those that are informed by the Guiding Principles.

5 The Cultural Proficiency Continuum

Changing the Conversation

> *Being able to put aside one's self-centered focus and impulses has social benefits: It opens the way to empathy, to real listening, to taking another person's perspective. Empathy . . . leads to caring, altruism, and compassion. Seeing things from another's perspective breaks down biased stereotypes, and so breeds tolerance and acceptance of differences. These capacities are ever more called on in our increasingly pluralistic society, allowing people to live together in mutual respect and creating the possibility of productive public discourse. These are the basic arts of democracy.*
>
> —Daniel Goleman (1995, p. 285)

We send emotional signals in every encounter, and those signals affect the people we are with whether we are aware of our impact. Conscious attention to how our behavior makes another person feel—for instance, sad, rejected, scared, and incompetent or happy, accepted, safe, and productive—are examples of interpersonal competence that enables us to interact with other people effectively and responsively. Self-management combined with empathy for others helps us to analyze and control our own emotional dispositions and reactions and our resulting behaviors in terms of both their personal and their social benefit. These basic social competences or "people skills" enable us to shape effective interactions, make meaningful connections, and recognize and respond to people's feelings and concerns. More than ever before, the growing diversity and increasing pluralism of our schools require educational leaders to be socially competent in ways that demonstrate respect, mutual understanding, justice, and concern for students who are culturally unlike them—students who differ racially and ethnically, students who speak different languages, students who have different beliefs, and students who have different ways of expressing their cultural distinctiveness.

Educational leaders may not know every important aspect of each of the diverse cultures represented in most American public schools today. The culturally proficient response to this dilemma is to seek and develop the knowledge, skills, and attitudes that demonstrate openness and authentic responsiveness to the heritage, values, and expressions of each cultural group represented in the student population. To lead successfully now, as discussed in Chapter 4, leaders also must consistently model socially competent attitudes, values, and dispositions by demonstrating interactions that are shaped by understanding and embracing the principles of Cultural Proficiency as core leadership values.

Understanding and acknowledging the Guiding Principles of Cultural Proficiency, described in Chapter 4, and choosing to manifest them in your behaviors are demonstrations of culturally proficient leadership. The choice you make to align your leadership actions with the Guiding Principles of Cultural Proficiency communicates a strong message throughout your school's community that you value diversity and fully expect that every individual will do the same. Indeed, the Guiding Principles are attitudinal benchmarks that enable you and others to assess progress toward acknowledging and valuing cultural differences, and although this assessment yields crucial information, it is insufficient by itself in provoking the development of culturally proficient behaviors.

CULTURAL PROFICIENCY: A TRANSFORMATIVE APPROACH

Cultural Proficiency is an inside-out perspective on change in which school leaders transform approaches to their personal leadership behaviors and to their school practices. Leaders who manifest Cultural Proficiency guide their colleagues to examine personal values and behaviors in such a way that the members of the school realize that it is they who must adapt their practices to meet the needs of the students and the community they serve. Likewise, these leaders support their colleagues and members of the community in aligning the school's policies, practices, and procedures to achieve Cultural Proficiency (Lindsey, Nuri Robins, & Terrell, 2003, 2009; Nuri Robins, Lindsey, Lindsey, & Terrell, 2002).

THE CULTURAL PROFICIENCY CONTINUUM

As a leader, making a commitment to align your practice with culturally proficient behavior and working to engage others in making similar commitments require that you begin where you are—individually and organizationally. The Cultural Proficiency Continuum is a tool that offers you a contextual frame of reference that is useful in examining and analyzing your responses to issues that arise from diverse environments. From an organizational perspective, the Continuum provides a means of assessing how your school or district deals with cultural differences. It also can assist you and others in examining and evaluating how your organization initiates, implements, and enforces policies and practices that represent its position on issues of diversity.

The Continuum describes a range of behaviors from *destructiveness*, the denial and suppression of a people's culture, to *proficiency*, the acknowledgment and elevation of all cultures (see Figure 5.1). The behaviors identified on the Continuum are not fixed points; rather, each descriptive point represents an array of practices and policies that characterize a developmental stage or phase of social competence.

As an educational leader, you must recognize that responses and reactions to students' cultural identities have a profound influence on what students learn and how they learn it. Furthermore, a leader's responses and reactions to difference, whether conscious or unconscious, can be manifested in several ways that range from devastating a student's sense of cultural identity to maximizing and enlarging a student's uniqueness. The range of these responses is represented in the Cultural Proficiency Continuum (Cross, 1989; Lindsey, Nuri Robins, & Terrell, 1999, 2003, 2009):

Figure 5.1 The Cultural Proficiency Continuum

Cultural Destructiveness		Cultural Blindness		Cultural Competence	
	Cultural Incapacity		Cultural Precompetence		Cultural Proficiency

- *Cultural destructiveness:* negating, disparaging, or purging cultures that are different from your own.
- *Cultural incapacity:* elevating the superiority of your own cultural values and beliefs and suppressing cultures that are different from your own.
- *Cultural blindness:* acting as if differences among cultures do not exist and refusing to recognize any differences.
- *Cultural precompetence:* recognizing that lack of knowledge, experience, and understanding of other cultures limits your ability to effectively interact with them.
- *Cultural competence:* employing any policy, practice, or behavior that uses the Essential Elements of Cultural Proficiency on behalf of the school or the district. Cultural competence is interacting with other cultural groups in ways that recognize and value their differences, motivate you to assess your own skills, expand your knowledge and resources, and, ultimately, cause you to adapt your relational behavior.
- *Cultural Proficiency:* advocating in ways that honor the differences among cultures, seeing diversity as a benefit, and interacting knowledgeably and respectfully among a variety of cultural groups.

The Continuum can be useful and instructive as a tool to assess growth toward Cultural Proficiency. Used as a gauge, it can yield a realistic appraisal of both your personal and your organizational development toward proficient cultural practices. Most important, the Continuum can help you determine where to begin—that is, where you are. To begin with yourself is an inside-out process of self-examination, evaluation, and awareness. In such a process, you become self-conscious in the best sense. To begin with yourself calls on you to make an authentic assessment of your assumptions, attitudes, dispositions, and behaviors. Which phase on the Continuum would best characterize your stage of development? What about your organization? Where along the Continuum would you place your organization's (school's or district's) policies and practices? The complexity of the task is hidden in the simplicity of the question.

Reflective Activity

Become self-conscious. Consider how you respond and react to displays of cultural distinctiveness and expression that are different from your own sense of cultural identity. Think of a recent situation during which you encountered such an experience. What signals did you communicate?

_____

_____

Movement along the Continuum will not be a smooth journey on which you glide continually forward in the right direction. Your progress toward competence and proficiency, like your learning, may be a rocky, bumpy ride at times. Sometimes you will lurch forward and then slide backward, sometimes you may stall, and sometimes the road will smooth out before you and you will make great progress. The decision to learn and grow and change is yours to make.

RETURN TO MAPLE VIEW

In the following brief episodes, we return to the Maple View School District to examine some everyday school interactions that illustrate the six points of the Continuum. The situations described are simulations of authentic experiences we have had in schools in which we have worked. Following each of the interactions is a set of questions that will guide you in your learning at three levels: Analyze the vignette, describe the behavior, and identify the underlying assumptions implicit in the particular situation.

Episode 1: It's Not My Job!

> *Cultural destructiveness* is any action that negates, disparages, or purges cultural practices or expressions of culture that are different from your own; it may be manifested through an organization's policies and practices or through an individual's assumptions and behavior.

Cultural destructiveness has its basis in historical acts of oppression, whether racism, sexism, heterosexism, or any other "-ism." The history of our country has been one of a slowly unfolding democracy. Initially, voting and property rights were almost solely the domains of propertied white men. The struggles to eliminate African slavery, Native American apartheid, Jim Crow segregation, Japanese American internment, and the subjugation of women to second-class status are among the many vital parts of our history that are rarely visible in our schools' curricula. The effect of this omission is twofold. First, it deprives educators and their students of a context by which to understand the disparities that exist in today's schools (Loewen, 1995, 2009). Without this context for understanding the disparities that exist in society, it is too easy to ascribe cause to being a lack of initiative or will. Second, it fails to "show the numerous benefits that members of the dominant group have derived from the subjugation of other people" (Nuri Robins, Lindsey, Lindsey, & Terrell, 2012, p. 80).

Whether intentional or not, the effect of culturally destructive school leaders' behaviors or schools' practices has the effect of denying nondominant groups legitimacy in the school setting. Blatant racist, sexist, or heterosexist behaviors and school policies and practices are, no doubt, rarely visible to most educators. However, there are behaviors, policies, and practices that create and perpetuate disparate treatment in our classrooms and schools that are invisible to the educator but are quite obvious to those most directly affected by the acts. It is this latter set of behaviors and policies that are addressed in the first episode.

The first situation involves members of the faculty at Maple View Middle School who are working with Alfredo Crawford, a recognized expert in instructional strategies for English language acquisition. As you read this episode, look for the indications of culturally destructive behavior and the assumptions that such behavior reveals.

Maple View Middle School has been experiencing demographic shifts in its student population for the past several years. Many of the students now attending the school are identified as English learning students. Faced with this new reality, some teachers have taken the initiative to earn second-language instruction authorizations. In most cases, the recently credentialed teachers learned effective second-language instructional strategies through their university coursework. They have inspired some of the more experienced teachers to use the new, more effective techniques. However, there is some resistance, as you will see by this conversation at a recent staff development session.

Dr. Crawford was beginning to introduce an activity in today's professional development session when Ira Robinson, a seventh-grade math instructor, stood up with his arms folded across his chest. In an argumentative tone, but with a smile on his face, Ira interjects:

Ira Robinson:	Mr. Crawford, or is it Dr. Crawford? Are you going to tell us again that we're not doing our jobs here—that is, we're not doing a good job?
Alfredo Crawford:	Well, first please call me "Alfredo" or "Mr. Crawford" or "Dr. Crawford." I'm comfortable with any of them. Now, what makes you think I am going to criticize your work?
Ira:	We hear it every time they bring somebody in to talk to us. Ever since the students began to change, all we've heard around here is that we're doing a lousy job. We hear it every year from the principal when the test scores come out. But

never, never do we hear what the parents need to do. They're the ones who are responsible.

Alfredo: I hear a lot of frustration in what you're saying, Ira—or . . . Mr. Robinson. What I plan to do today is share some interesting new strategies and approaches that should make your teaching more effective and remove some of that frustration you're feeling.

Ira (sitting down angrily): Well, Dr. Crawford, I find that insulting! I've been teaching math here for 23 years, and you're going to tell me that I know what I'm doing. The problem isn't my teaching "strategy," as you put it. The problem is these kids who don't speak English. I know how to teach math. I'm not an English teacher.

Alfredo (standing silently for a moment): When you and I earned our teaching credentials, there were relatively few immigrant students in our schools. During careers, that has changed substantially. Now we've got the responsibility to teach students who have limited or no English skills.

Ira: Well, there are a lot of us here who don't believe it's our job to be an induction center for immigrants. If these people want to be in this country, let them learn the language before coming here! As for me, I'm a math teacher. It's not my job to teach English, or for that matter, what you call "language acquisition skills."

Reflective Activity

How is cultural destructiveness displayed in this vignette? What is the culturally destructive behavior?

_____

_____

_____

_____

What assumptions is Mr. Robinson making?

_____

_____

_____

_____

As the school's principal, how would you seek to mediate this situation?

_____

_____

_____

_____

Episode 2: Shiny Red Apples

Cultural incapacity is any action that elevates the superiority of your own cultural values and beliefs while suppressing cultures that are different from your own.

Cultural incapacity is any policy, practice, or behavior that venerates one culture over all others. Such policies, practices, or behaviors can influence the worldviews of members of both the dominant and the nondominant groups. The history of our country is replete with examples of official acts of cultural incapacity, such as the restrictive immigration and Jim Crow laws of the 19th and 20th centuries. Laws such as these helped systematize the belief in the superiority of the dominant group and the inherent inferiority of subordinate groups. The combination of laws and concomitant beliefs among members of the dominant group gives rise to discriminatory practices, lowered expectations, and subtle messages to people that they are not valued (Nuri Robins et al., 2012). Freire (1987, 1999) discussed the net effect of these behavior and practices as being internalized oppression when members of nondominant groups assume the worldview of the dominant group to be true.

In the previous discussion of cultural destructiveness, we pointed out that the negative effect of a behavior, practice, or policy that is demeaning had little or no relationship to one's intentionality. The same is true for cultural incapacity. To the student, parent, community member, or colleague, when a person becomes an object and not a fully functioning person through another person's prejudice, bias, stereotyping, or indifference, it all feels the same. The net effect for the person on the receiving end of the behavior, practice, or policy may range from anger to resistance and learned helplessness.

In the second situation, we visit the classroom of Mrs. Dorothy Jackson, a teacher at Maple View Elementary School who, along with other teachers at the school, has been working with Dr. Laura Ruiz, a reading and language arts consultant from the regional Comprehensive School Reform Center. As you read this episode, look for the indications of behavior that culturally incapacitates specific groups of students, and identify the assumptions that this behavior reveals.

Dr. Ruiz has asked Anne Browning, the Maple View School District's language arts coordinator, to accompany her on today's visit to Maple View Elementary. Dr. Ruiz has been working with the teachers in grade-level groups to help them improve their writing instruction. The school's Latino and African American students, particularly the boys in these groups, have not demonstrated adequate progress in English composition and generative writing skills. She is spending the week visiting class-rooms. Last week, she met with the school's leadership team and agreed with them that she should familiarize herself with the culture of the school and classrooms to be most helpful in coaching teachers to strengthen their writing programs and improve their instructional strategies. Today, we go along with Laura and Anne as they begin their visit to Dorothy Jackson's fourth-grade classroom.

Laura and Anne arrive at the classroom at approximately 10 a.m. and find it abuzz with activity. As she enters the classroom, Laura quickly scans the environment for examples of students' work. A colorful bulletin board on the rear wall displays a large apple tree made of construction paper. On one side of the tree is a heading that reads "The Red Apples," and on the other side is a heading that reads "The Green Apples." Laura observes that both sides display apples with children's names on them, and she wonders what criteria are used to determine the placement of apples.

As the two visitors enter the classroom, Dorothy Jackson interrupts the class to introduce Dr. Ruiz and Ms. Browning to the students:

Dorothy (greeting the two visitors at the door and smiling in a welcoming way):	Class, this is Dr. Ruiz and Ms. Browning. Dr. Ruiz is the person I was telling you about. She is going to help us improve our writing here at Maple View. If you recall, yesterday I told you that Dr. Ruiz was going to visit our classroom and watch how we learn to write. Remember?
Laura (smiling and walking into the classroom):	Good morning, class. Mrs. Jackson is right. I'm here to learn from you by observing how you do your writing and watching to see what helps you learn. I don't want to interrupt you, so please go back to your work. Ms. Browning and I will be very quiet so that we don't bother you. (The two women walk to the rear of the classroom.)
Dorothy:	Well, first Dr. Ruiz and Ms. Browning, let me intro-duce my wonderful fourth graders. We are working on a writing assignment this morning. These stu-dents (gesturing to a group of girls) are my shining

red apples. They have already finished the assignment and are doing some enrichment work. Their
stories are just wonderful. This group (gesturing to
another group of mostly Latino and African
American boys) we call the green apples. They have
a long way to go before they turn red. This is the
group that needs your help.

Laura's heart sank as she listened to Dorothy's introduction. She
glanced at Anne and saw that she also was disturbed by the teacher's
words. The students carried on with their work as if nothing unusual had
occurred. The effect of Dorothy's comments may not be readily discernible
in the moment, but most assuredly, they will have a cumulative effect on
both groups of students.

Reflective Activity

How is cultural incapacity displayed in this episode? What is the culturally incapacitating behavior? Who is incapacitated?

_____

_____

_____

_____

How would you describe the expectations Mrs. Jackson has of her learners? What information reveals her expectations?

_____

_____

_____

_____

How might different groups of students in Mrs. Jackson's class judge their
own capabilities? Why?

_____

_____

_____

_____

As a school leader, how would you work with Mrs. Jackson?

_____

_____

_____

_____

Episode 3: They All Look Alike to Me

Cultural blindness is any policy, practice, or behavior that ignores existing cultural differences or that considers such differences inconsequential.

Cultural blindness is a vexing point on the Continuum in that there is often a difference between what is stated and how the statement is experienced. Blindness is in the speaker not being able to hear how others are receiving the statements. Blindness is in the speaker being mystified or angry that he or she was misunderstood. The dominant culture in our country has placed a high value on cultural blindness. You can see it in many of our instructional materials. When there are faces of color, they are most often in the context of middle-class and upper-middle-class experiences. Similarly, much of our history and language arts materials revolve around heroic themes that show how people have benefited from struggles as if all one had to do to overcome one's lot in life was to work a little harder or, at least, not be so sensitive.

The third situation involves Maureen Bailey, the newly appointed principal at Rose Garden Elementary School, who is meeting with her faculty group after visiting every classroom in the school. The Rose Garden faculty has been working together for the past five years to create an interdisciplinary project-based curriculum that integrates language arts and social studies. As you read this episode, look for the indications of behavior that ignores existing cultural differences among groups of students and the assumptions that this behavior reveals.

Maureen Bailey has had the good fortune to have served as an educator in several different settings. She began as a teacher in the Department of Defense Schools, which gave her many exciting opportunities to teach in Western Europe, Turkey, Korea, and Central America. For the past eight years, she has worked in the Maple View School District, first as a teacher for five years and later as an assistant principal. This year, she has been promoted to the position of principal at Rose Garden Elementary School, one of the older school facilities in Maple View. Rose Garden is located on the east side of the district and draws students from a community that is richly diverse both culturally and economically. The school has earned a reputation throughout the county for its tradition of recognizing, respecting, and celebrating the many racial, socio-cultural, and linguistic customs and traditions of its students and their families.

During the past five years, the teachers at Rose Garden have worked together in grade-level clusters to develop a schoolwide project-based language arts and social studies curriculum that engages students in learning and applying content standards within the context of their own and other students' heritages. Many parents—even those who have full-time jobs—volunteer their time and contribute traditional artifacts so that students can learn about diverse cultures from authentic sources. Rose Garden's curriculum is exemplary, and many teachers from other districts visit the school to observe how the teachers plan and develop their innovative curriculum in teams and how they use the curriculum with their students.

Soon after school resumed in September, Maureen announced to the faculty that she would be visiting each classroom, attending every curriculum-planning meeting, speaking with each teacher, and interviewing some students to learn more about what was going on in the school. Now, on an afternoon in early October, Maureen has chosen her third meeting with the faculty to share her observations. The faculty has gathered in the school's library to hear her report:

Maureen Bailey (standing in front of the group holding a sheaf of papers):	I'm so happy to be the principal at this school! You're all such professionals, and you're doing such good work with these children—even with all the challenges you face every day.
Maxine Cho (raising her hand and then speaking when Maureen acknowledges her):	Thanks, Maureen! I'm impressed that you made it to every classroom already. But what I really want to know is: What's your impression of the rich diversity at this school? I mean, as you visited the classrooms, what were some of the things students from different ethnic groups were doing? What impressions did you take away from that?
Maureen:	Well, when I look at the school as a whole, the diversity is incredible. But, I think what I've noticed most, after visiting every classroom and watching the students doing their work, is that I can't tell you the ethnic, racial, or gender makeup of the students in your classrooms. I really don't see color. They all look like good little Americans to me, and I think that's great!

Maxine (stunned and silent for several seconds):	Mrs. Bailey, I'm surprised to hear your response. As you know, here at Rose Garden we have been working extremely hard to acknowledge and respect each of the groups represented in our student population. We are committed to recognizing the unique characteristics and contributions of each of the groups represented in our student population.

Reflective Activity

How is cultural blindness displayed in this episode? Why is this culturally blind behavior?

_____

_____

_____

_____

What are the assumptions that underlie this cultural blindness?

_____

_____

_____

_____

In what ways is cultural blindness a deterrent to successful learning?

_____

_____

_____

_____

How might you advise or coach Maxine Cho and the other teachers in the school to respond to Maureen Bailey? Why?

_____

_____

_____

_____

As a district leader, how would you work with Maureen?

_____

_____

_____

_____

Episode 4: No Excuses

> *Culturally precompetent* people and organizations recognize that their skills and practices are limited when interacting with other cultural groups.

Cultural precompetence occurs as people beginning to discover what they don't know. The culturally precompetent educator has at least a basic understanding of his or her own culture and the awareness that his or her school has a distinct organizational culture. The culturally precompetent educator has begun the shift from talking about educational disparities as something being wrong with *them* to *our practice* needing to be adapted for use with new groups. The culturally precompetent educator has begun to see that the dominant group is handicapped in what it does not know about interacting with groups other than their own. Very often, a hallmark of the culturally precompetent educator is frustration in knowing that current practices are not effective but not knowing what to do about it. This can be a point of readiness where educators are ready to engage in their own learning.

The fourth situation portrays a group of teachers on the academic planning team at Maple View High School. For several weeks, they have been meeting with Connie Hampton, Maple View's assistant principal, to review and analyze their latest student performance data in relation to their expectations for their students. As you read this episode, look for the indications of members of the group beginning to realize their limitations regarding their students' backgrounds and cultural experiences. What are the assumptions this behavior reveals?

Ten years ago, Maple View High School was recognized as having one of the most "rigorous" secondary academic programs in the county. Test scores have declined steadily during the past decade. Many in the school district cite the shift in student demographics as being the cause for the decline in test scores. The student body now consists of recent immigrants from Mexico, Central America, Asia, and Middle Eastern countries. Fewer than half of the students are from middle-income families, and most others are from lower-income families, for which opportunities for formal education have been limited.

The school's administrators, in an effort to provide support for immigrant students, gradually dropped much of their rigorous curriculum in favor of an increasing number of English as a second language and remedial math classes. They believed that students must be proficient in English and basic computation skills to be successful in this country. However, the scores continued the downward trend.

A small core of rigorous courses and "advanced placement" classes were continuing to serve approximately 18% of the students who were able to meet the high expectations of their teachers. This small cluster of students could compete academically with students from any other high school in the county, and they were the source of much school pride on the part of the school's administrators. The downward cycle of test scores caused the school to qualify for state funds to address the needs of students. The academic planning team, in consultation with an external evaluator, has been engaged in examining student test scores along with other indicators of student achievement.

Today, Dr. Hampton is meeting with the teachers on the team, and she is just completing a guided review of the test scores for the past three years. This is the third session in which the academic planning team has been examining these data:

Connie Hampton (turning off the overhead projector):	Okay, we've been looking at these data for over three weeks now, and we've been looking at the ways the school's curriculum meets or doesn't meet the needs of all of our students. What patterns are you seeing today?
Josh Turner (a young biology teacher, quickly responds):	Well, the first time we looked at all these reports, I wondered to myself: Wow, how can we expect anything different from kids whose parents don't value education? Now, I am at a different place.
Irene Thompson (school counselor and chair of the faculty senate):	Me, too, and I can't figure out why and where. It seems so strange.
Josh:	Well, I've been thinking a lot about a question you asked at our last meeting, Connie. You asked us something like—let me know if I get this right.
Connie:	I will, Josh. Go on.
Josh:	Okay, last week, when we were looking at the family background data, I said I thought many of our parents are poorly educated. You agreed, but followed with, "What can you do differently that will make a difference in our students' learning?" Somehow, it doesn't seem like you responded to my comment. Am I missing something?

Irene:	Yes, that's what I heard, too!
Connie:	So, Josh and Irene, you both heard my question, and you've been thinking about it all week. What did that question mean for you?
Josh (smiling a little anxiously):	Well, this isn't very comfortable, and it won't be, but the past week I've been thinking that we're the ones who have to change what we're doing if we want our students to learn what we expect them to learn.
Irene (nodding in agreement):	Do you remember what you said at our first meeting, Connie? I've been thinking about it a lot. You said there are no excuses for not teaching our students. I've been thinking about that. "No excuses" means we have to find new ways to teach our students what they need to know.
Josh:	Yes, that's what's been rattling around in my brain all week, too. We have no excuses.

Reflective Activity

How is cultural precompetence displayed in this episode? What are Josh and Irene learning?

_____

_____

_____

_____

How would you describe the expectations that Connie Hampton has for the teachers at Maple View High? What information reveals her expectations?

_____

_____

_____

_____

If you were Connie, how would you continue working with Josh and Irene and the other teachers in the group?

_____

_____

_____

_____

What do you see as the challenges for this group, and how would you coach them?

_____

_____

_____

_____

Episode 5: Bridges Among Cultures

Cultural competence is any policy, practice, or behavior that uses the Essential Elements of Cultural Proficiency for the individual or the organization. The Essential Elements are as follows:

- Assessing culture
- Valuing diversity
- Managing the dynamics of difference
- Adapting to diversity
- Institutionalizing cultural knowledge

Culturally competent school leaders use the Guiding Principles as beacons and the five Essential Elements as standards for their personal and organizational planning. These leaders are students of themselves and the culture of their schools. Culturally competent school leaders take the responsibility and opportunity to use the five Essential Elements as leverage points for improving current practices so that educators, students, parents, and community members are in an environment in which continuous improvement is fundamental to the school vision.

The fifth episode depicts the work of a district task force that is assessing and analyzing the district's middle school social studies curriculum. Maple View's superintendent, Dr. Sam Brewer, has selected Anthony (Tony) Franklin, the principal at Pine Hills Middle School, to chair the district's Middle Grades Social Studies Standards Task Force. Dr. Brewer wants Tony and the other members of the task force to assess how well the district's middle school social studies curriculum aligns with the state's Social Studies Standards. He also has asked the task force for an assessment of how well the district's and the state's standards align with the

principles of Cultural Proficiency that are guiding all curriculum development in the district. The task force includes new and experienced teachers,
two administrators, a school counselor, and parents from the district's
Community Cultural Proficiency Council. As you read this episode, watch
for indications of behavior that demonstrate cultural competence. What
evidence of cultural competence can you find in the episode?

Today's task force session is the second meeting for the group. Sitting
around the table today are Tony, the chair; Helene Kim, a seventh-grade
history teacher; Jackie Sims, a sixth-grade social studies teacher in her second year; Francisco Alvarado, the assistant principal at Maple View Middle
School; Lucy Tyrell, the counselor at Pine Hills Middle School; and Kwame
Randolph, the parent of two middle school students at Maple View and
cochair of the Community Cultural Proficiency Council. They are waiting
for a few more task force members before they begin. Tony is energized and
anxious to get the meeting started. He has brought copies of the standards
along with copies of the Guiding Principles of Cultural Proficiency:

Tony Franklin (distributing the copies around the table):	I'd like to get started. We have a lot to do, and this is a very important task, one that is going to take considerable time and study.
Helene Kim (nodding in agreement):	You're so right, Tony. I feel very honored to be on this task force.
Jackie Sims:	Oh, me too. And as a new teacher, I'm so grateful for the opportunity to work with all of you on this important task. I'm so pleased to have Lucy on our team. Lucy has been a social studies teacher at both Pine Hills and Maple View. In her role as counselor, she remains the one most knowledgeable about the breadth and depth of our curriculum.
Helene:	She's also on the district's Community Cultural Proficiency Council.
Kwame Randolph (agreeing with Helene):	It seems to me that a good beginning might be to hear Lucy's assessment of our district curriculum. So, Lucy, just how balanced is our curriculum? In other words, what do you see as our strong points, and what are the points of omission?
Lucy Tyrell (after a moment of reflection):	I'm very comfortable with that as a starting point, but I want to let you know that I've got blind spots, too. For instance, the events of September 11 and those that continue to emerge have shown me how little I know about the Middle East, the Muslim religion, or our

country's formal and informal policies that impact these issues. One of the things I see coming from this study is that even though our district has no Middle Eastern or Muslim students that I'm aware of, how important it is for our curriculum to be inclusive.

Francisco Alvarado: Yes, the emerging Common Core State Standards for social studies are very explicit about our students being prepared to live and function in an interdependent, global world. Lucy, I'm sure that your blind spot is one that many of us share. That kind of openness is what we need as we begin this work.

Lucy: You're so right, Francisco. We need to make sure that our district's social studies curriculum builds bridges for our students to learn about and recognize the many diverse cultural groups among us.

Tony (smiling broadly): That's it! That's what our work is all about. We're building bridges among us, among our cultures.

Reflective Activity

How is culturally competent behavior displayed in this episode? What example stands out for you?

_____

_____

_____

_____

What are some of the assumptions held by participants in this episode? What evidence is included in the episode?

_____

_____

_____

_____

What do you think Dr. Sam Brewer envisions as the next steps for this group? If you had the opportunity, how might you coach him?

_____

_____

_____

_____

Episode 6: Change Your Calendar

Cultural Proficiency is knowing how to learn and teach about different groups in ways that acknowledge and honor all people and the
groups they represent.

Cultural Proficiency is a way of being alert and aware as a leader. Cultural
Proficiency is manifest in organizations and people who esteem cultures,
who continually learn about individuals and organizational cultures, and
who interact effectively with a variety of cultural groups. The culturally proficient leader acknowledges the interrelatedness of personal, organizational,
and cultural learning. Advocacy is a distinguishing characteristic of the culturally proficient leader. The culturally proficient leader advocates for people
because it is the right and moral thing to do irrespective of whether or not the
subjects of the advocacy are in the room at the time.

The school leadership team at Maple View Middle School was working
with the assistant principal, Francisco Alvarado, to generate a curriculum-
planning calendar. To have accurate information for the calendar, they
decided to track and monitor the attendance patterns of all their students
to schedule important curriculum units during the times of the year when
most of the students are present. As you read this episode, look for examples of culturally proficient behavior among the team members.

Among several distinct patterns, the team's data revealed that many
students of Mexican ancestry, especially those who had come to the United
States recently, were absent around the times of cultural events such as
Christmas and Easter. The pattern showed that for the past several years,
large numbers of students and their families had regularly returned to
Mexico to visit their families and celebrate religious and other cultural
events. It was not unusual for students to return from Christmas and Easter
visits with families in Mexico having missed a total of three weeks of classroom work, a situation that placed them far behind other students. This
situation too often caused misery for both the students and the teachers.

The administrators and teachers at Maple View had asked the parents
to not take their children out of school for such long periods of time. The
school had worked with parents to help them understand the educational
practices of their new country so that they would have their children back
when school resumed. The strong cultural pull of family celebrations
seemed to be stronger than the cultural tradition of the school calendar.
The teachers even tried creating homework alternatives so the children

could keep up with their schoolwork during these important family events. Their efforts were met with mixed results.

Today, the team is meeting to assess the results of their campaign to keep students in their classrooms. Sarah Chainey, a sixth-grade science teacher, is facilitating the meeting. Other members of the team include Helene Kim, a seventh-grade social studies teacher; Ron Sumii, an eighth-grade algebra teacher; and Jocelyn Donaldson, a seventh-grade language arts teacher. Francisco Alvarado, the school's assistant principal, also joined the group:

Sarah Chainey (displaying an overhead of the data):	So, as you see here, we've had this pattern of student absences every December and April. It's so frustrating because the kids are missing out on so much.
Ron Sumii:	Yep! The kids are right on target through the fall and into December. Then, bam, they're gone for three weeks. They fall behind and they never catch up. Their parents need to respect our school calendar.
Francisco Alvarado:	Sarah, you say the kids are missing out on so much. What would they miss if they didn't go back to Mexico to visit their families? For these kids, family is the center of their culture.
Jocelyn Donaldson:	I think you're right, Francisco. What if we change our calendar? Is that a possibility? Can we do that?
Francisco:	Our school calendar has to be 183 school days. Working with that total, we could organize our calendar so that the kids wouldn't fall behind in their schoolwork.
Sarah (turning off the projector):	Jocelyn, you're brilliant!
Helene Kim:	Wait, Sarah. Put that overhead up again. We can use it to plot our new calendar.
Ron:	That's right. Now let's see, we need to plot our 183 days around these two blocks of time when the kids are in Mexico.

Finally, it occurred to the leadership team that the school was organized around the living patterns of students and families who had long ago migrated from the area. They decided they that could demonstrate respect for the families in the school's attendance area and organize the school calendar around their lifestyles, in much the same way their predecessors had generations before. With this new insight, the leadership team proposed that the school calendar be organized to fit the lifestyle patterns of the families the school was serving. Now, the school is closed for winter break for 4 weeks in late December and early January and for two weeks during the observance of Passion and Easter weeks. Once the decision was made and the calendar change was instituted, Sarah Chainey was heard explaining the Maple View teacher's accomplishment to a group of teachers from another school:

> You know, once we decided that the school calendar was created by people to serve their needs generations ago and was not etched in stone, it was pretty easy to get our priorities in order and decide how we could best meet the needs of our communities. Pretty neat, huh!

Reflective Activity

How is culturally proficient behavior depicted in this episode? What is one small, individual example you can describe?

_____

_____

_____

_____

How do the assumptions of the participants in this episode shift? What stimulates the shift?

_____

_____

_____

_____

If you were coaching this team, what next steps would you advise them to take?

_____

_____

_____

_____

What do you envision for this team as they continue their progress toward becoming culturally proficient?

_____

_____

_____

_____

In Chapters 3, 4, and 5, you have become acquainted with three important tools: the Barriers, Guiding Principles, and the Cultural Proficiency
Continuum. Chapter 6 will guide you toward a deeper understanding of
culturally proficient behavior by introducing the five Essential Elements of
Cultural Competence. Before you move on, take a few moments to reflect
on your own goals in relation to becoming more culturally proficient. What
do you want your behavior to communicate to others? What signals do you
want to send to people whose cultural identity is different from yours?

_____

_____

_____

_____

 # The Essential Elements as Standards for Leadership Behavior

In order to progress toward this goal, several current assumptions about equity and schooling must be challenged and changed to move the focus from diversity to equity and from tolerance to transformation.

—Stephanie Graham (2002, p. 21)

Culturally competent school leaders understand that effective leadership in a diverse environment is about changing the manner in which we work with those who are culturally different from ourselves. Personal transformation that facilitates organizational change is the goal of Cultural Proficiency.

Leading effectively in a diverse environment is *not* about changing others; *it is about our own personal work.* To guide the personal work in which school leaders examine their own values and behaviors and, in due time, the policies and practices of the school, the five Essential Elements of Cultural Competence serve as *standards* for culturally competent leadership. The Essential Elements of culturally competent school leadership are as follows (Lindsey, Jungwirth, Pahl, & Lindsey, 2009; Nuri Robins, Lindsey, Lindsey, & Terrell 2002):

- Assesses Culture: *identify the differences among the people in your environment.*
- Values Diversity: *embrace the differences as contributing to the value of the environment.*
- Manages the Dynamics of Difference: *reframe the differences so that diversity is not perceived as a problem to be solved.*
- Adapts to Diversity: *teach and learn about differences and how to respond to them effectively.*
- Institutionalize Cultural Knowledge: *change the systems to ensure healthy and effective responses to diversity.*

As you read this chapter, review the assumptions for each point of the Continuum that you identified in Chapter 5. Reviewing those assumptions will serve you in two ways. First, in reflecting on your assumptions, you will better understand the behaviors along the Continuum and develop an even deeper appreciation for how our decisions as school leaders affect students. Second, after reading this chapter, you will know if your assumptions are consistent with the standards embodied in the five Essential Elements of Cultural Competence. At that point, you will have the opportunity to be intentional in choosing to integrate the Essential Elements into your professional practice.

The Cultural Proficiency Continuum is composed of six points. The three points to the left side of the Continuum focus on the behaviors and perceived motivation of others, while the three points to the right side of the Continuum focus on personal behaviors and our motives as school leaders. Importantly, the transition between Cultural Blindness and Cultural Precompetence serves as a tipping point, or *shift in thinking* (Gladwell, 2000). As leaders, a shift in thinking occurs when we turn our attention

- **from** our interpretation of the behavior and motivation of others
- **to** an introspective look at our own behavior, values and motives.

The conversations move from what to do about "them" to what can we do to effect change in ways that better meet the needs of our students and their communities. When experiencing this shift in thinking, school leaders examine their and the district's policies and practices to discover or devise ways in which to better serve their diverse communities. School leaders with whom we have worked describe this shift as being from the paralysis associated with cultural blindness to the empowerment involved with examining their own practices as school leaders.

TOLERANCE FOR DIVERSITY VERSUS TRANSFORMATION FOR EQUITY

During school years 1999 and 2000, nine superintendents from Los Angeles and San Bernardino Counties met to study the achievement gap within their schools. They invited the equity consultant from the Los Angeles County Office of Education and an author of this book to serve as resource persons and to facilitate the meetings. In time, they assumed the title of *Superintendents' Collaborative for School Equity and Achievement*. These superintendents were very knowledgeable about the dynamics affecting the achievement gap. They knew that having low-achieving students simply *work harder* was not the answer to closing the achievement gap. They knew that the answer to closing the achievement gap involved the intricate interplay of educator and system *assumptions, expectations,* and *cultural issues* (Graham & Lindsey, 2002).

In adapting the Cultural Proficiency approach to devising ways to close the achievement gap, the members of the Superintendents' Collaborative made clear distinctions in their use of the five Essential Elements of Cultural Competence. The frame the superintendents created was to move from the more traditional viewpoint of *tolerance for diversity* to *personal and institutional transformation for equity.* Table 6.1 illustrates their summary of how the superintendents represented the five Essential Elements as *transformative change,* as seen with the descriptors in the right column. Conversely, they illustrated corresponding descriptors for change in the left column that represent what it looks like when one *tolerates change.*

Moving from the conventional perspective of tolerance for diversity to the perspective of educational leaders, who intentionally seek equity, was an engaging process involving a commitment of time and energy. The group met in a series of three-hour sessions held at six-week intervals. The superintendents considered many issues that might close gaps in equity and achievement and, ultimately, decided on three outcomes for their work:

- As educational leaders, they would view issues of cultural power to be central, not ancillary, to student success.
- As educational leaders, they would develop a protocol for changing personal and organizational paradigms for school equity and achievement.
- As educational leaders, they would renew their commitment to the moral purposes of education, which are *to make a positive difference in the lives of all citizens,* and to show individuals how to function together in a society (Graham & Lindsey, 2002).

The superintendents immersed themselves in readings about organization change including systems theory, organization reframing, and

Table 6.1 The Five Essential Elements as Leverage Points for Change

FROM: TOLERANCE FOR DIVERSITY *Destructiveness, Incapacity &* *Blindness* The focus is on *them*.	TO: TRANSFORMATION FOR EQUITY *Precompetence, Competence &* *Proficiency* The focus is on *our practices*.
Assessing One's Own Cultural Knowledge—Demographics are viewed as a challenge	**Assessing One's Own Cultural Knowledge**—Demographics are used to inform policy and practice
Valuing Diversity—Tolerate, assimilate, acculturate	**Valuing Diversity**—Esteem, respect, adapt
Managing the Dynamics of Difference—Prevent, mitigate, avoid	**Managing the Dynamics of Difference**—Manage, leverage, facilitate
Adapting to Diversity—Systemwide accountability to meet changing needs of a diverse community and reduce cultural dissonance and conflict.	**Adapting to Diversity**—Systemwide accountability for continuous improvement and responsiveness to community. Staff understands, operates and perseveres on the edge of often rapid and continuous change.
Institutionalizing Cultural Knowledge—Information contributed or added to existing policies, procedures, practices	**Institutionalizing Cultural Knowledge**—Information integrated into system, provoking significant changes to policies, procedures, practices

transformational leadership. They read and discussed current articles on standards-based accountability. They examined and discussed student achievement data in each of their districts and posed questions to one another about how the district might be contributing to poor student performance. They concluded their study by constructing a comprehensive policy statement for equity, *Transforming Systems for Cultural Proficiency: Changing Personal and Organizational Paradigms for School Equity and Achievement* (Graham & Lindsey, 2002).

The central part of their policy statement involved arranging the Cultural Proficiency Continuum into its two prominent components, the three points to the left side of the Continuum—Destructiveness, Incapacity, Blindness—that focus on the behaviors of others; and the three points to the right side of the Continuum—Precompetence, Competence, Proficiency—that focus on the behaviors of educators.

We selected this example of collaboration to demonstrate the bold steps these superintendents took in identifying initiatives for closing the achievement gap among students in their school districts. The shift in thinking that occurred among these chief executives was to examine school leadership practices. Talma Moore-Stuart, principal at Pine Hills High School, kept this shift in thinking in mind as he and Dr. Stephanie Barnes, the school improvement coach, began to work with the school leadership team to identify obstacles to student achievement at the high school.

PINE HILLS HIGH SCHOOL'S LEADERSHIP APPROACH TO CULTURAL PROFICIENCY

Culturally Proficient leaders are intentional in their own learning. Dr. Brewer realized that when he told the principals that he expected an analysis of the obstacles that seem to be getting in the way of the academic and social success of each demographic group of students. Talma Moore-Stuart, the principal at Pine Hills High School, has been working with her school leadership team to develop their capacity in working with the concepts of Cultural Proficiency. Dr. Stephanie Barnes, the school improvement coach, and five teachers comprised the school leadership team. The teachers were Rob Moore, Joel Peters, Jack Thompson, Janice Thompson, and Maxine Parks.

Mrs. Moore-Stuart had taken to heart the notion that a culturally precompetent leader is aware of what she does not know and that she is willing and ready to learn. She and members of the school leadership team had committed considerable time to studying the Guiding Principles and the Cultural Proficiency Continuum. They were now ready to use the five Essential Elements of Cultural Competence as standards and indicators for their planning. Talma distributed copies of the set of tables that comprised the *Superintendents' Collaborative for School Equity and Achievement*. She indicated that the tables represented each of the Essential Elements described as standards for culturally competent leadership.

ESSENTIAL ELEMENTS AS STANDARDS FOR LEADERSHIP BEHAVIOR AND SCHOOL POLICY

Tables 6.1 through 6.7 represent leadership behaviors for each of the Essential Elements of Cultural Competence. You will read how the school leadership team at Pine Hills High School chose to use the information in the tables. The information in the tables represents leadership actions taken in schools and provides you with clear choices to guide or assess decision making.

Talma Moore-Stuart:	As our school's leadership team, it is going to be our responsibility to do the initial planning to move our school toward Cultural Proficiency.
Rob Moore:	I don't argue with the direction, but I am not certain how you intend that to occur? The Guiding Principles and the Continuum information were interesting and helpful, but where do we go from here?
Maxine Parks:	Yeah, based on my understanding of the Continuum, I can see the big picture, but I, too, can't see how we go about doing it. I know it has to do with the set of five standards, or Essential Elements.
Stephanie Barnes:	Precisely! Let me begin by sharing with you the format for our planning. From there, I will review with you the five elements as leadership standards for our work. (Stephanie distributes a one-page handout in chart form.) It is necessary for us to take what Dr. Brewer is calling Bold Steps. Consider these question, as represented in this handout:
Rob:	So, how would you like to proceed?

BOLD STEPS TOWARD CULTURAL PROFICIENCY

- What would Cultural Proficiency look like at your school?
- What are chief challenges you face in putting some of these into action at your school site?
- In light of the team's understanding of Cultural Proficiency, what are our values and beliefs as a team?
- Based on our values and beliefs, what *Three Bold Steps* are we able to take as a team that would embrace the Principles of Cultural Proficiency at our school sites/district?
- What conditions for success will put these *Three Bold Steps* in place?

Talma:	I would like for us to do as we did at the district leadership team meeting which is to have each of us respond individually to these statements and, then, to discuss and synthesize our thinking.
Maxine:	Well, this sure looks compelling! How do we get there?
Stephanie (laughing):	Yes, it is compelling and before we get to this planning piece, successfully using it will require us to examine both our own motivation and the underlying assumptions of why we do the things we do.

Joe Peters:	What do you mean by, "Why we do the things we do?"
Sam:	Remember, the opportunity is for us to adapt our practices in such a way that our students have greater success, both academically and socially. In doing that, each of us will have to examine our assumptions about our students, about the curriculum we select, about the manner in which we teach, and how we interact with our community. What do we believe about what we do?
Janice Thompson:	Ahhhh. I am beginning to see what "inside-out" learning means.
Rob:	Yeah, me too! Now I clearly see that **my** learning is about **my** underlying assumptions and **our** learning is about **our** practices.

We invite you to review the assumptions for each point of the Continuum that you identified in Chapter 5. Reviewing those assumptions will serve you in two ways. First, in reflecting on your assumptions and reading the tables and text in this chapter, you better understand the behaviors along the Continuum and have an even deeper appreciation for how our decisions as school leaders affect students. Second, you now know if your assumptions are consistent with the standards embodied in the five Essential Elements of Cultural Competence. Now you can be intentional in integrating the Essential Elements into your professional practice.

Now that you have reviewed the information in Table 6.1, The Five Essential Elements as Leverage Points for Change, we invite you to reflect on your planning. Take a few minutes and reflect on the assumptions you listed in Chapter 5. Consider what planning for Cultural Proficiency means for you and your school. Use the following prompts to describe *the bold steps you are willing to take for you, and your school, to be culturally proficient.* After completing your responses, please proceed to read Tables 6.2 through 6.6 that describe the five Essential Elements that serve as standards for Culturally Competent Leadership.

Reflective Activity: Bold Steps Toward Cultural Proficiency

What would Cultural Proficiency look like at your school?

_____

_____

_____

_____

What are chief challenges you face in putting some of these into action at your site/district?

_____

_____

_____

_____

In light of your school team's understanding of the Guiding Principles of Cultural Proficiency, what are your team's values and beliefs?

_____

_____

_____

_____

Based on your team's values and beliefs, what *Three Bold Steps* are you able to take as a team that will embrace the principles of Cultural Proficiency at your school sites/district?

_____

_____

_____

_____

What conditions for success are necessary to put these *Three Bold Steps* in place?

_____

_____

_____

_____

MAKING SENSE OF THE ELEMENTS, STANDARDS, AND BEHAVIOR

Members of the Pine Hills High school leadership team began to study each of the Essential Elements, expressed as standards, and to show how each represented the shift from a tolerance for diversity versus a transformation for equity perspective. Listen to the members of the team as they begin to read the five standards as Essential Elements of Cultural Competence and use the tables for assessing their behaviors and school practices.

Stephanie:	Please keep in mind that these five standards for Culturally Competent Leadership compose one of the Tools of Cultural Proficiency.
Joel:	You know, I do understand that each of the Essential Elements serves as leadership standards for planning, but it would sure be helpful to have some greater in-depth information about them. I, for one, am fed up with all of that theory malarkey. I want concrete examples!
Janice:	Stephanie, you know what the standards and elements look like in practice. Is that what these tables are supposed to do for us?
Stephanie:	Yes, I think it best if we take a concerted look at each of the Essential Elements. They will be helpful as we proceed with our work.
Talma:	Good point! I think members of the team will find this information provocative on one hand and highly informative on the other. You will see some of our current practices cast in a negative light. I encourage you to keep an open mind, to read the standard carefully, and to examine the practices on the right-hand side of each table.

In Table 6.2, the activity of Assessing Culture is represented in the two phases of the Cultural Proficiency Continuum. Take a few minutes and read each of the five tables, 6.2 to 6.6, carefully. First, read the standard and be certain you understand the culturally competent leadership behavior described. Then, read the contrasting behaviors represented in each of the tables. In each case, the descriptions in the left column are of behaviors that focus outward on others as being the problem whereas the behaviors in the right column focus on empowering change of personal practice. Personal leadership involves working with others to achieve a goal or purpose. Educational leaders who work with colleagues on issues related to teaching and learning are, in fact, focusing their attention on personal practice. Leaders' practice involves those actions that support educators' acquiring the knowledge and skills they need to be successful with their students. As you read each of the standards and tables, notice what administrators and teachers would need to do to focus on their respective educational practices.

Assesses Culture: *Identify the differences among the people in your environment.* A school leader promotes the success of all students by facilitating an examination of one's own culture, and the effect it may have on others in the school, and learning about the cultures that compose the community in which the school resides. The school leader

- recognizes her culture and its effects on others;
- describes her own culture norms and the cultural norms of her organization; and
- understands how the culture of her school affects those with different cultures served by the school.

This standard introduces the notion of the inside-out approach to change. The focus is within, whether it is the administrator, the counselor, the teacher, the grade level, the department, the school, or the district. The culturally proficient leader is introspective and is interested to know the effect that his culture has on others. He studies the culture—operating values, assumptions, and beliefs—of his school and its grade levels or departments. Leaders use the insights gained from personal introspection and examination of the school culture to help others acclimatize to the school community. He facilitates transformative change within the school that invites others to become part of an ever-evolving school organization.

Table 6.2 represents the two phases of the Cultural Proficiency Continuum. The leader behaviors in the left column portray behaviors that tolerate diversity reflective of changing demographics. Leadership behaviors in the right column are the leadership behaviors demonstrated when the examination of professional practices leads to professional and personal transformation.

Maxine:	Hmmm, this first one is interesting. Where did it come from?
Talma:	They were developed by a group of superintendents in the Los Angeles area who decided they wanted to find ways to close the achievement gap.
Janice:	Wow, this first table (6.2) is busy!
Maxine:	Yeah, it sure is.
Talma:	Well, what do you see?
Janice:	Several things! First, as you can see, one's leadership skills become more appropriate as you move from the left column to the right column.
Joel:	This could be very uncomfortable for some people!
Rob:	What do you mean?
Joel:	What I mean is it is very possible I could find a decision or attitude I have that appears negative on this Continuum.

Table 6.2 Leadership Behaviors for Assessing One's Own Culture

FROM: **TOLERANCE FOR DIVERSITY** *Destructiveness, Incapacity &* *Blindness* **The focus is on *them*.**	*TO:* **TRANSFORMATION FOR EQUITY** *Precompetence, Competence &* *Proficiency* **The focus is on *our practices*.**
When assessing one's and the school's culture, the leader views changing demographics as a threat or challenge. He	When assessing one's own and the school's culture, the leader studies demographics to inform policy and practice. She
• upholds practices that present changing demographics to be barriers/obstacles to current educational practice, organization, funding, governance, systemwide effectiveness, and accountability;	• analyzes demographic data to assess their cultural knowledge and to examine the mismatch between the intent of the system and the outcomes for clients served;
• implements policies that maintains that students, their families, languages, class, race/ethnicity, and neighborhoods are academic, social, and economic deficits and in need of intervention and remediation; and	• implements policies in which students, their families, languages, race/ethnicity, and neighborhoods are used as resources to enhance the way the school provides resources to ensure high expectations and the attainment of rigorous standards for all; and
• presents reform as driven by external audits, compliance reviews, litigation, or threat of sanctions from funding or oversight agencies (state departments of education, U.S. Department of Education, Office of Civil Rights, U.S. Department of Justice, American Civil Liberties Union, etc.).	• initiates transformative change driven by higher moral purpose—to make a democracy possible, to make a positive difference in the lives of students, and to teach individuals how they can function effectively and together in a society that embraces diversity.

Sam: That is the beauty of this table. If you find a behavior or attitude that reflects a decision or belief of yours, you can see other choices you have. Remember, cultural competence is about being intentional with one's behavior.

Maxine: That's helpful!

Stephanie: Good, because this deepens our understanding of the element.

Janice and Joel nod in agreement.

Rob: You know, Talma, as I continue to look at this table, I see a lot of our behaviors at this school not being what I want for us!

Jack: Such as?

Rob: Well, I have been here for 22 years and in that time, we have had a major demographic shift in our student population and community. I am willing to bet that some of these illustrations about the school not changing do apply to us. Also, our increased reliance on discipline. Whooee, this is going to be interesting!

Maxine: Yes, but the redeeming feature is that we have illustrations for more appropriate choices. It is really helpful to see concrete illustrations. As I look at the remaining four tables, I can readily see how they will be helpful as we continue our planning.

Stephanie: Let's take a look at the content in the next four standards.

Values Diversity: *Embrace the differences as contributing to the value of the environment.* A school leader welcomes diversity into the school by developing a community of learning within the school and with parents and other interested members of the school community. The school leader

- states that tolerance is an initial step on the way to valuing diversity and stresses embracing diversity as the end goal;
- celebrates and encourages the presence of a variety of people in all activities in order to maximize perspective and experiences;
- recognizes differences as diversity rather than as inappropriate responses to the school community; and
- accepts that each culture finds some values and behaviors more important than others do.

School administrators and other school leaders have the moral responsibility to set a positive tone for valuing diversity in schools. For too long, we have turned a blind eye to the different experiences students have in our schools. One of the constructive features of the accountability movement is that we now have the opportunity to examine demographic-group data. The wide use of data is one of the great revolutions of 21st century schools. We readily gather data, and array it by demographic groupings, to learn how academically and socially successful our students are. However, the data, in and of itself, is not liberating. It is the perspective that we take to the data that permits us to be effective in working cross-culturally. This becomes the moral responsibility of school leaders, whether administrators or teachers. Fullan (2003) sets forth criteria that address the moral purpose of schools:

- That all students and teachers benefit in terms of identified desirable goals
- That the gap between high and low performers becomes less as the bar for all is raised
- That ever-deeper educational goals are pursued
- That the culture of the school becomes so transformed that continuous improvement relative to the previous three components becomes built in (p. 31)

In Table 6.3, you see contrasting phases of valuing diversity along the Cultural Proficiency Continuum. Take note of how the behaviors in the left column serve to abdicate our responsibility while the behaviors in the right column are proactive in ways that cause us to examine our educational practices.

Manages the Dynamics of Difference: *Reframe the differences so that diversity is not perceived as a problem to be solved.* A school leader recognizes that conflict is a natural and normal part of life and learns to manage conflict to the best interest of all involved. She recognizes conflict as constrained energy needing proper release into the system. The school leader

- learns and uses effective facilitation strategies for resolving conflict, particularly among people whose cultural backgrounds and values differ;
- understands the effect that historic distrust has on present-day interactions; and
- realizes that one may misjudge others' actions based on learned expectations.

School administrators and other school leaders can create a constructive and instructive environment for managing conflict. Conflict is natural and normal in human relationships and within any organization, even in so-called homogeneous communities. Schools are complex organizations composed of different educator roles, parents with whom to relate, political interactions with regulatory agencies, and varied community constituent groups. Then, when we add racial, ethnic, gender, social class, religious, and sexual orientation diversity issues, we have real schools in real communities. In these diverse settings, managing the dynamics of difference is about how conflict can deepen understanding among cultural groups. An educational leader who values diversity uses the current situation to provide others with the information and skills that inform one

Table 6.3 Leadership Behaviors for Valuing Diversity

FROM: **TOLERANCE FOR DIVERSITY** *Destructiveness, Incapacity &* *Blindness* **The focus is on** *them.*	*TO:* **TRANSFORMATION FOR EQUITY** *Precompetence, Competence &* *Proficiency* **The focus is on** *our practices.*
When the leader encounters cultures different from hers, her approach is to tolerate, assimilate, and acculturate. She	When encountering cultures different from his, the leader's approach to diversity is to value, esteem, respect, and adapt. He
• states that *others* are the products of an educational, socioeconomic, or cultural deficit, and she focuses the school system in helping them to assimilate while she leads the effort to maintain the cultural/educational status quo;	• sponsors an inside-out systemic approach that leads the system, and individuals within it, to examine how well student/community needs are being met and then adapts so multiple voices are heard and integrated into the formulation of policy and practice;
• employs standards-based accountability systems that discount knowledge from nondominant groups; that excludes some learning and communication styles; and, which may have punitive effects on underserved students; and	• uses standards to ensure high expectations for all, differentiated instruction, multiple assessment and resources ensuring success of students to achieve rigorous academic standards; and
• uses professional development training to focus on understanding *others* and improving communication with *them.*	• facilitates professional learning that focuses on understanding of self and how to identify and remove existing barriers to equitable education.

another of our respective histories, languages, lifestyles, and worldviews (Nuri Robins, Lindsey, Lindsey, & Terrell, 2012) She further facilitates school community members in developing mutual operating norms that bond organization relationships.

Table 6.4 represents the behaviors of managing the dynamics of difference in the two phases of the Cultural Proficiency Continuum. Culturally proficient behaviors are representative of the personal transformation that occurs when one assumes responsibility for her behavior.

Table 6.4 Leadership Behaviors for Managing the Dynamics of Difference

FROM:	*TO:*
TOLERANCE FOR DIVERSITY	**TRANSFORMATION FOR EQUITY**
Destructiveness, Incapacity & *Blindness*	*Precompetence, Competence &* *Proficiency*
The focus is on *them*.	**The focus is on *our practices*.**
When dealing with conflict that arises from cross-cultural contact, the leader's response is to prevent, mitigate, and avoid. He	**When dealing with conflict that arises from cross-cultural contact, the leader's response is to manage, leverage, and facilitate. She**
• avoids dissonant, controversial topics and issues;	• facilitates, challenges, and provokes positive conflict and discussion about difficult topics and issues;
• seeks commonalities through early agreement and consensus to unite divided/diverse groups. Difference is viewed as threatening, risky, and divisive;	• seeks difference rather than commonality by helping the group to learn from dissonance and to forge new, more complex agreements and capabilities that transform the organization to be able to respond to multiple perspectives and voices;
• expresses the assumption that the system is fair for everyone if the rules are followed. He calls attention to the good intentions of individuals in the system. He assumes those who are different (e.g., race, gender, sexual orientation, socioeconomic class, religion, age) are judged and treated fairly;	• acknowledges historical inequity for some groups. She openly recognizes one's own agentry as a beneficiary of race, gender, orientation, class, religion, or age privilege;
• states that populations not experiencing conflict do not need training or development for Cultural Proficiency; and	• states that homogeneous populations need training and development for Cultural Proficiency to ensure that silence or passivity does not mask repressed conflict; and
• recruits, hires, and promotes individuals who are like-minded.	• recruits, hires, and promotes people who think and act differently from those already in the system.

Adapts to Diversity: *Teach and learn about differences and how to respond to them effectively.* A school leader promotes continuous learning with his school and community colleagues to mitigate issues arising from differences in experiences and perspectives. The school leader

- changes the current way of doing things to acknowledge the differences that are present in the staff, clients, and community;
- develops skills to facilitate intercultural communication; and
- institutionalizes cultural interventions for conflicts and confusion caused by the dynamics of difference.

To adapt to diversity is first to recognize that everyone changes and that change is ongoing. Faculties change as teachers, counselors, and administrators leave and new people take their places. Communities change as people leave for new lives elsewhere and new families take their places. Quite often, those changes include the cultural compositions of schools. We expect school leaders, irrespective of the demographic profile of the school, to ensure the success of students of all cultural groups and from all parts of the community. As new groups of people move into the community or as gaps in student success are identified, the educational leaders are responsible for the initial learning. They have the responsibility to learn about the histories, languages, lifestyles, and worldviews of the people who are new to the school.

This initial learning is fundamental to adaptation. Adapting to diversity is the embodiment of change as a process in which school leaders have made a personal and institutional commitment to that process. The culturally proficient leader uses his knowledge about the new members of the community, in combination with his skills in managing the dynamics of difference, to educate his staff members. It is his responsibility to impart the new knowledge and skills in such a way that the faculty will learn the respective histories, languages, lifestyles, and worldviews of the changing community.

Table 6.5 represents the behavior of adapting to diversity at the two phases of the Cultural Proficiency Continuum. As in the previous tables, the behaviors in the left column describe tolerating diversity, and the behaviors in the right column describe initiatives leaders take when committing to serving the needs of the total community.

Institutionalize Cultural Knowledge: *Change the systems to ensure healthy and effective responses to diversity.* A school leader provides opportunities for school and community colleagues to use information about the school and community cultures in ways that honor and challenge continuous learning. The school leader

Table 6.5 Leadership Behaviors for Adapting to Diversity

FROM: **TOLERANCE FOR DIVERSITY** *Destructiveness, Incapacity &* *Blindness* The focus is on *them.*	*TO:* **TRANSFORMATION FOR EQUITY** *Precompetence, Competence &* *Proficiency* The focus is on *our practices.*
Leaders respond to systemwide accountability intended to meet the needs of a changing, diverse community and take action to reduce cultural dissonance and conflict.	Leaders use systemwide accountability for continuous improvement and responsiveness to community. Staff members understand, operate, and persevere on the edge of often rapid and continuous change.
As the leader, he	As the leader, she
• develops and uses multiple programs to meet multiple goals. The organization monitors resource allocation and accountability to funding source;	• integrates important themes, programs, and goals. Resources are combined and allocated equitably to students and communities most in need;
• invests in recruiting and hiring new staff members who are competent, committed, and caring;	• invests, at the district level, in capacity building of staff that is competent, committed, and caring;
• has a laserlike focus on high expectations and achievement and an orientation for timely intervention and remediation for students not making progress; and	• has a laserlike focus on high expectations and achievement and an orientation for prevention of student learning gaps; and
• holds teachers accountable for high standards for all students and high-quality instruction based on standards.	• holds teachers, administrators, staff, parents, and students accountable for high standards and quality instruction. Stakeholders ensure that standards-based instruction and accountability for test scores do not result in diminished educational quality or negative educational consequences for any student/student groups.

- incorporates cultural knowledge into the mainstream of the organization;
- teaches the origins of stereotypes and prejudices; and
- integrates into school systems information and skills that enable all to interact effectively in a variety of intercultural situations.

Educational leaders, administrators, counselors, or teachers are the managers of cultural knowledge. It is within their domain of power to decide what is to be included. The key components of *institutionalizing cultural knowledge* are learning about your own culture and the culture of your own school (or grade level or department) and learning how each group experiences the school (Nuri Robins et al., 2002). Whether the current initiative is an increasingly diverse faculty or it is examining the disaggregated data of student achievement, culturally proficient leaders facilitate professional learning that demonstrates a commitment to life-long learning. The culturally proficient leader works hard not to dichotomize learning. She infuses the learning with new knowledge and skills about technology, standards, and curriculum with an ever-deeper understanding of how people learn and transmit their cultural values. In Chapter 8, you will learn a template for leading in a culture of transformative change.

Table 6.6 is more detailed than the other tables in this chapter. The categories in this table represent prominent leadership actions to institutionalize cultural knowledge—curriculum and instruction, assessment, training and professional development, and parent communication/community outreach. As with the previous examples, the behaviors in the left column represent additive actions that have the effect of tolerance. In contrast, the behaviors in the right column represent personal leadership and organizational transformation.

The five Essential Elements of Cultural Proficiency serve as standards by which leaders and school leadership teams can guide their work. The school leadership team at Pine Hills High School has completed its initial review of the five tables. Let's listen to the team's conversation.

Stephanie: Well, what do you think?

There are several minutes of silence. Then, Rob speaks,

Rob: I am a little speechless, a little angry, a little hopeful—a lot confused!

Sam: It is not easy, is it?

Janice: I won't try to speak for Rob, but this is intimidating. I found our examination of the Guiding Principles to be challenging. For me, the Continuum was eye opening. But this is a lot!

Stephanie: What do you mean, "a lot?"

Janice: Well, as someone said earlier, I find a lot of my and the school's behaviors on the left side of these tables. I am not sure I agree in all cases.

Table 6.6 Leadership Behaviors for Institutionalizing Cultural Knowledge

FROM: **TOLERANCE FOR DIVERSITY** *Destructiveness, Incapacity &* *Blindness* The focus is on *them.*	*TO:* **TRANSFORMATION FOR EQUITY** *Precompetence, Competence &* *Proficiency* The focus is on *our practices.*
Information is added to existing policies, procedures, and practices.	**Information is integrated into the system, provoking significant changes to policies, procedures, and practices.**
A. **Curriculum and Instruction**—The leader adds to current practice, in that she • employs the use of rigorous standards to drive curriculum; alternate curriculum/curricular paths or remedial interventions are provided for underperforming students; • adds multicultural content, activities, and resources to the curriculum and/or she sponsors school programs to acknowledge the contributions of racial, ethnic, and cultural groups; and • schedules multicultural/ diversity programs for students and/or staff that focus on understanding others, conflict resolution, behavior management tolerance, and character education.	A. **Curriculum and Instruction**—The leader fosters change in the system, in that he • uses rigorous standards-driven curriculum consistent with Common Core State Standards in which teachers use scaffolding and research-based strategies to ensure all student progress toward standards; • integrates multiple perspectives about topics, issues, themes, and events into the curriculum. Textbooks and other resources accurately and positively portray cultural/ethnic/racial/gender groups; and • focuses on ones's own Cultural Proficiency to facilitate the use of multicultural/diversity programs for students and staff to help the organization identify and remove barriers to achievement for all students.
B. **Assessment**—The leader adds to current practice, in that she • uses only assessment procedures and methods that are tightly controlled by nationally normed tests;	B. **Assessment**—The leader fosters change in the system, in that he • uses school/classroom assessment procedures that are openly shared, flexible, and do not dominate curriculum and instruction;

(Continued)

Table 6.6 (Continued)

• schedules instructional time to be spent on *test-prep* for tests that have high-stakes consequences for some students;	• ensures that students have multiple, varied opportunities to demonstrate progress. Assessment strategies support students in demonstrating what they know and guide them to improve and expand their learning;
• requires teachers to provide alternate intervention/ remediation, often in pullout programs, for students not making progress toward standards;	• disaggregates data and frequently uses formative assessments with teachers to plan, monitor, and adjust instruction and to provide specific feedback about progress toward clear learning targets that support grade-level content standards;
• confines primary users of assessment to be teachers and school/district staff members;	• involves students and parents in assessing student achievement;
• uses rubrics to ensure consistent, fair assessment of student work; and	• shares and uses rubrics as instructional tools to articulate learning targets and standards to all; and
• has students with special needs waived out of many schoolwide assessments.	• makes accommodations to maximize success for students with special needs.
C. **Training and Professional Development**—The leader adds to current practice, in that she	C. **Professional Learning**—The leader facilitates change in the system, in that he
• sponsors professional development that is compliance driven. Participation is often mandatory;	• sponsors professional learning seminars driven by the desire to transform the self, first, in order to develop the organization's Cultural Proficiency.
• promotes multicultural education designed to heighten feelings of inclusion for minority students, to help all students understand each other better, and to reduce conflict and violence on school campuses. Those closest to the students	• uses long-term, systemwide equity-based diversity training to identify and remove barriers to achievement and that requires all staff members and stakeholders to professionally engage in processes that provoke dialogue, challenge assumptions, and catalyze change

Table 6.6 (Continued)

(teachers and support staff members) are the primary audience for multicultural education/diversity training; and	for individuals and the organization. Those responsible for facilitating changes at all levels of the system are the primary audience; and
• designs and implements professional development outcomes that result in the addition of multicultural units to the curriculum, the addition of multicultural artifacts on display in classrooms and the school, and the addition of multicultural celebrations and assemblies to the extracurricular program.	• designs and implements training outcomes to result in the creation of curriculum in which students value other cultural groups. Individual and organizational changes result in closing the gaps in achievement, performance, and success experienced disproportionately by members of some student groups.
D. Parent Communication/ Community Outreach—The leader adds to current practice, in that she	**D. Parent Communication/Community Outreach**—The leader fosters change in the system, in that he
• encourages parents to share cultural information, artifacts, and traditions to enrich school programs;	• involves parents from multiple cultural groups as active collaborators in school/district decision making. The school communicates in the language of the parents/community, providing interpreters, child care, food, transportation, and so on. Alternate meeting times and locations meet the needs of the community. Meeting agendas address community issues and concerns;
• solicits parents to participate on school advisory committees, especially those committees that address concerns of specific cultural groups; and	• involves parents as partners in important decisions that affect their children's education; and
• seeks information for educators and staff members that promotes understanding about community cultures through multiple information resources and school/district orientations and training sessions.	• has all staff members interact with families at school events and in local community settings to gain and generate authentic information and understanding about community cultures.

Sam: Well, let's eat this elephant one bite at a time.

Joel: Yes, that is a good idea. Like Rob and Janice, I had the same initial reaction to the tables. But, as I continue to look at them, the information on the right side of the tables does seem to make sense.

Maxine: I agree. What is interesting to me is how these examples really make our earlier discussions of the Guiding Principles come alive for me.

Stephanie: Are you ready to move forward?

All nod in agreement, though seemingly some appear to be feeling dissonant.

Stephanie: To assist us in this planning, Dr. Brewer has devised a template for strategic planning for Cultural Competence to help us in doing this work. It is titled "Template—Strategic Planning for Cultural Proficiency."

TEMPLATE FOR STRATEGIC PLANNING

Educators motivated to become culturally proficient do so with moral intent and, often, in the face of resistance within their schools and districts. Whether you undertake this journey to follow your own values and beliefs or if you are working with a team, strategic planning is critical. Table 6.7, *Template—Strategic Planning for Cultural Proficiency*, is for you to use in combination with Tables 6.1 to 6.6.

Tables 6.1 to 6.6 provide you and your colleagues with detailed examples of culturally proficient behaviors in the columns to the right in each chart. The columns to the left in each chart provide you with illustrations of behaviors that you will want to reconsider their use if they describe how you currently do things in your school. The template in Table 6.7 provides you with a framework for recording your selected leadership actions, the person(s) responsible for the actions, and the agreed-upon timeline.

Once again, we invite you to review the assumptions for each point on the Continuum that you identified in Chapter 5. Reviewing those assumptions will serve you in two ways. First, in reflecting on your assumptions and reading the tables and text in this chapter, you better understand the behaviors along the Continuum and have an even deeper appreciation for how our decisions as school leaders affect students. Second, you now know if your assumptions are consistent with the standards embodied in the five Essential Elements of Cultural Proficiency.

Table 6.7 Template—Strategic Planning for Cultural Proficiency

Essential Element	What Leadership Action Is to Be Taken?	Who Will Do It?	By When?
Assessing Cultural Knowledge			
Valuing Diversity			
Managing the Dynamics of Difference			
Adapting to Diversity			
Institutionalizing Cultural Knowledge: • Curriculum and Instruction • Assessment • Professional Learning Seminars/ Opportunities • Parent and Community Engagement			

Now you can be intentional in integrating the Essential Elements into your professional practice.

GOING DEEPER

Now that you have completed your reading and study of the Tools of Cultural Proficiency, in what ways do you see them supporting your role as an educator? In what ways might the Tools inform and support the work in your school? Please use the space below to record your responses.

_____

_____

_____

_____

Chapters 3 through 6 have provided you with the tools of culturally competent practice and the opportunity to reflect on your own practice. Part III, Chapters 7 and 8, provide you with techniques and tools to use in professional development. Chapter 7 provides an overview of the forms of conversation we use in our schools and an activity to use in professional development sessions with your colleagues. Chapter 8 describes a lab protocol you and your colleagues can use to ingrain the Tools of Cultural Proficiency into everyday practice.

Author's Note: Subsequent to the publishing of the first edition of this book, Stephanie, Randy and two colleagues developed a set of rubrics that evolved from the tables presented in this chapter. For more information, you may want to refer to Randall B. Lindsey, Stephanie M. Graham, R. Chris Westphal, Jr., & Cynthia L. Jew. (2008). *Culturally proficient inquiry: A lens for identifying and examining educational gaps*. Thousand Oaks, Corwin.

Part III

Professional Learning for Organizational Change

In the first two sections of this book, you took an in-depth tour of the Tools of Cultural Proficiency. In Part I, you explored how Cultural Proficiency undergirds efforts to eliminate a lingering gap in academic achievement among demographic student groups. You reviewed historical legacy of generational poverty and systemic oppression maintained through legislative, legal, and economic means and their effect on our schools today. Part II acquainted you with the Tools of Cultural Proficiency and highlighted their usefulness as instruments for educators in meeting the educational challenges of today. The Cultural Proficiency Conceptual Framework illustrated the manner in which the four Tools of Cultural Proficiency promote and support equitable educational practice. Chapters 3 through 6 guided you through detailed examination of each of the Tools of Cultural Proficiency—Barriers, Guiding Principles, Continuum, and Essential Elements.

Part III provides practical applications for cultivating organizational relationships that enhance professional learning. Schools are complex organizations consisting of intricate webs of relationships nestled within the belief systems of their educators. Culturally proficient school leaders develop dynamic processes and structures that facilitate professional learning that fits into the natural webs of these networks. Relationship building through cocreative processes inherent in conversation is presented as an important element in developing culturally proficient schools responsive to the academic and social needs of diverse and ever-changing communities. In Chapter 7, we provide rationale for the art and possibility of dialogue as a key strategic element to culturally proficient professional learning. We present a conversational protocol for assessing the deep moral and ethical structures held by organization members. The process of assessing a school's policies and procedures leads members to clarify their behaviors that either inhibit or support school reform and change. Chapter 8 extends the investigation of culturally proficient professional learning to the collegial structure of the Learning Lab. With the Lab you will learn detailed steps for a comprehensive methodology that critically challenges deeply held assumptions and harvests educational structures foundational to intentional, moral leadership actions toward equitable change that benefits all students.

7 Conversation

A Skill for the Culturally Proficient Leader

Listening . . . requires not only open eyes and ears, but open hearts and minds. We do not really see through our eyes or hear through our ears, but through our beliefs. . . . It is not easy, but it is the only way to learn what it might feel like to be someone else and the only way to start the dialogue.

—Lisa Delpit (1995, p. 46)

GETTING CENTERED

Take a few moments and consider your professional learning goals for the near future. Describe what you consider as your communication strengths. In what area of communication would you like to grow? To what extent do you consider yourself effective in cross-cultural communications? What might be areas of growth in cross-cultural communications for you?

_____

_____

_____

_____

SKILLFUL USE OF COMMUNICATION CHANNELS

Dr. Sam Brewer and his colleagues set forth a vision for the Maple View School District to commit its effort and resources to provide a high-quality education for all students that enables each one to achieve or exceed high academic and performance standards. Dr. Brewer committed to leading the district to examine behaviors and policies through the lens of Cultural Proficiency. In Chapters 3 through 6, we have had the opportunity to witness many conversations of Maple View educators and community members as they have learned the basic Tools of Cultural Proficiency—the Barriers of anger and guilt, the Guiding Principles, the Continuum, and the Essential Elements.

In the vignettes of the preceding chapters, we have learned that culturally proficient leaders are intentional in the use of their school's formal and informal communication networks. These leaders, who are both administrators and teachers, are aware of the power of person-to-person communication. They understand that building effective relationships involves guiding their colleagues to understand the *whys* of individual and group behaviors. Once the *why* is clear—the moral imperative for all learners—the *what* and *how* become structurally effective. Culturally proficient leaders structure faculty meetings, department/grade-level meetings, and meetings with parents and community members in such a way as to maximize person-to-person communication. These same leaders realize that when they foster effective communication in their ongoing work, they are increasing the likelihood that the requisite skills and attitudes will carry over into the informal conversations among their colleagues. Culturally proficient school leaders see that relationship building through conversation is an important component in developing schools responsive to the needs of diverse and ever-changing communities.

In her powerful book *Coming Together*, Margaret Wheatley (2002) tells us that conversation is an ancient art form that comes naturally to us as humans, but that human beings are becoming increasingly isolated and fragmented and need one another more than ever. Schools often are isolating places in which dozens of adults spend 8 to 10 hours in relatively autonomous activities and interactions with their students but rarely spend time in effective conversations with other adults. Teachers are in their classrooms with 20 to 35 students while administrators and counselors are consumed with their daily tasks. Formal meetings and professional development sessions are frequently for one-way communication of information. Too often, we are in regimented situations that provide little time or opportunity to nurture deep, substantive conversations about our practices as educators.

Communication within schools occurs in both formal and informal settings. Formal settings include the aforementioned faculty meetings, parent-teacher meetings, grade-level and department meetings, as well as formal classroom instruction. Wenger (1998) has described our more informal communication networks in terms of *communities of practice.* Often, our communities of practice are composed of the networks of communication that occur in the hallways, the parking lots, the faculty lounge, or any other informal setting.

Conversation is one of the most important forms of social behavior in our schools, yet it receives little attention in either its formal or informal settings. Some conversation processes promote communication while others seemingly end in miscommunication or noncommunication. Cultural Proficiency requires understanding and mastery of the modes of conversation that promote effective communication—namely, raw debate, polite discussion, skilled discussion, and dialogue. In this chapter, we discuss conversation and its relationship to communication, understanding, and Cultural Proficiency. Later in this chapter, we present four modes of conversation described by Senge (1994) and describe how they relate to one another and how use of different modes of conversation to either promote or obstruct Cultural Proficiency in school settings. The chapter ends with exercises for dialogic practice designed to assist educational leaders who choose to move their schools and districts toward culturally proficient practices.

ORGANIZATIONS AS RELATIONSHIPS

Exploration of conversation as a means to becoming culturally proficient begins with an examination of the concept of organizations. Traditionally, we study organizations at two levels: structural and systemic (Cross, 1989, tOwens, 1995; Sergiovanni, 2001; Wheatley, 1992). Weick (1979) provides us with a **framework** for understanding the systemic nature of organizations:

> Most "things" in organizations are actually relationships, variables tied together in a systematic fashion. Events, therefore, depend on the strength of these ties, the direction of influence, the time it takes for information in the form of differences to move around circuits. (p. 88)

Viewing schools as relationships linked together as circuits is useful in understanding the interconnectedness of human social organizations and how information flows through them. Rather than schools being regarded only as building sites, Weick offers a view of organizations—in our case, schools—that are grounded in the values and beliefs of individuals. He states:

> The word *organization* is a noun, and it is also a myth. If you look for an organization you won't find it. What you will find is that there are events, linked together, that transpire within concrete walls and these sequences, their pathways, and their timing are the forms we errone- ously make into substances when we talk about an organization. Just as the skin is a misleading boundary for marking off where a person ends and the environment starts, so are the walls of an organization. Events inside organizations and organisms are locked into causal circuits that extend beyond these artificial boundaries. (p. 88)

Maturana and Varela (1992) extend our understanding of organiza- tions beyond the mechanics of linkages and circuits in relationships, toward an inward journey of life itself. They describe the organization of biological life, of which humans belong, as *autopoetic,* or self-organizing. The organization is a product of its own patterns, procedures, and pro- cesses and its responses or reactions to its environment and to external interactions. In other words, there is no separation between what it is and what it does:

> That living beings have an organization, of course, is proper not only to them but also to everything we can analyze as a system. What is distinctive about them, however, is that their organization is such that their only product is themselves, with no separation between producer and product. The being and doing of an autopoetic unity are inseparable and this is their specific mode of organization. (p. 48)

Organizations exist within the hearts and minds of the people who are part of them; they are the collective values and beliefs of those people. Organizational values and beliefs, in turn, are manifest in people's norma- tive actions. These actions comprise the agreed-upon inter-subjective real- ity of individuals that are experienced in the objective world, such as a place called school. When agreed-upon norms are breached in some fash- ion, conflict arises, which generates a struggle to reclaim the old norm by group members or insert a new one. For example, the goal of educating all children to high academic standards is a significant normative diversion from the prevalent educational practice of providing high standards for a select population of students.

> Conflicts in the domain of norm-guided interactions can be traced directly to some disruption of normative consensus. Repairing a disrupted consensus can mean one of two things: restoring inter-subjective recognition of a validity claim after it has become controversial or assuring inter-subjective recognition for a new validity claim that is a substitute for the old one. Agreement of this kind expresses a *common will*. (Habermas 1990, p. 67)

Efforts such as Race to the Top (American Recovery and Reinvestment Act of 2009) and the Common Core College and Career Readiness Standards (National Governors Association, 2010) are structural responses to a vision of a new society. However, what will be required to make this vision reality is the renegotiation of a consensual norm around who is to be educated. This renegotiation has to begin in the minds and hearts of those responsible for providing the education. Principals, teachers, counselors, and parents will need to engage in the struggle to discard the old norm of sorting and selecting students, reserving rigorous education for the "best and brightest," and agree to embrace a new norm of educating all to high academic standards.

Discarding an old norm and embracing a new one is a major task. It involves repairing a severe fracture in the bond around the old norm. This fracture engages the group in a crisis of legitimacy in the group's original purpose, causing fierce argument among group members as to the right or correct normative value that reestablishes group identity. At this juncture, members critically partake in the language process to renegotiate norms to bolster healthy relationships for a successful organization. At this point, language is not defined as a symbolic tool representing the surrounding world but as a medium through which we interpret and transform our realities. Herda (1999) provides this insight as to the utility of language:

> This medium brings us to the place of conversation and the domain of the text that gives us the capacity to redescribe or reconfigure our everyday world in organizations and communities. It is this redescription where social action, which moves beyond old behaviors and worn-out traditions, has its genesis. (p. 22)

Susan Scott (2004) aptly states, "The conversation is the relationship" (p. 6). Participating in what she refers to as "fierce conversation" is a key ingredient in sustaining healthy relationships and, by extension, organizations such as schools. Scott's notion of "fierce" is less frightening than it might seem at first glance. Participants are encouraged to approach conversations intensely, robustly, untamed, and unbridled. "In its simplest form," she states, "a fierce conversation is one in which we come out from behind ourselves into the conversation and make it real" (p. 7). Scott outlines seven principles for mastering the fierce conversation. A brief outline of each follows:

- *Principle 1: Master the courage to interrogate reality.*

  No plan survives its collision with reality, and reality has a habit of shifting, at work and at home.

- *Principle 2: Come out from behind yourself into the conversation and make it real.*

  While many fear "real," it is the unreal conversation that should scare us to death. When the conversation is real, the change occurs before the conversation is over.

- *Principle 3: Be here, prepared to be nowhere else.*

  Our work, our relationships, and our lives succeed or fail one conversation at a time. While no single conversation is guaranteed to transform a company, a relationship, or a life, any single conversation can.

- *Principle 4: Tackle your toughest challenge today.*

  Burnout doesn't occur because we're solving problems; it occurs because we've been trying to solve the same problem over and over.

- *Principle 5: Obey your instincts.*

  Don't just trust your instincts—obey them. Your radar works perfectly. It's the operator who is in question.

- *Principle 6: Take responsibility for your emotional wake.*

  For the leader, there is no trivial comment. Something you don't remember saying may have had a devastating impact on someone who looked to you for guidance and approval.

- *Principle 7: Let silence do the heavy lifting.*

  When there is simply a whole lot of talking going on, conversations can be so empty of meaning they crackle. Memorable conversations include breathing space. (p. xv)

Fierce and sometimes challenging conversations are commonplace in the culturally proficient school. Members of the school community readily critique their actions as a means of honing capacity to foster student achievement. Forms of conversation provide varying opportunities to coalesce people's values and beliefs, to shape collective understanding, to reveal people's underlying values and beliefs, and to open them to change. Often, however, members of the community get stuck and do not know how to respond when faced with culturally destructive, incapacitating, or blind comments or questions. Although walking away from the conversation may be easier, silence gives power and permission to the speakers of hurtful and harmful words of injustice. So, the question becomes, *If I stay, what will I say?* This question led one of our colleagues to develop Breakthrough Questions as a way to counter the downward spiral of negative conversations. Breakthrough Questions are formed by using one of the Essential Elements as the stem and building the question using the collaborative nature of learning communities. The downward spiral shifts to upward, positive energy through questions posed from positive intentionality, inclusive, and exploratory language (Lindsey, Jungwirth, Pahl, Jarvis, & Lindsey, 2009). Structures for developing Breakthrough Questions are included in the Resources section of this book. Structured conversations help prepare the speaker for the opportunity to critically examine moral attributes, leading to a culturally competent co-constructed space.

THE ESSENCE OF COMMUNICATION: CO-CONSTRUCTING MEANING

When people competently communicate with one another they authentically generate and share information. Meaning is consensually co-constructed, leading to more coherent bonds within relationships. This social construction of meaning is the essence of communication, and to understand it, we refer to a conversation between two Maple View Elementary teachers, Joan Stephens and Connie Barkley. Joan and Connie are talking about the Cultural Proficiency seminar in which they had recently participated. Joan was struggling to understand her deep emotional reactions to the session and asked Connie, a colleague she knew she could trust, to hear her out and help her make sense of her feelings.

In their conversation, Connie and Joan scrutinized their moral reference points relative to Cultural Proficiency as an appropriate perspective for addressing gaps in student achievement. Connie openly questioned Joan about contributions they both may have made to undereducating children. She gained permission from Joan to take the deeper plunge of critical inquiry in connection with their held values, assumptions, and beliefs about racism and the achievement gap. She steadfastly challenged her own sense of responsibility. This form of communication seeks understanding and hinges on the parties reaching an agreement on critical areas of concern among them.

Traditionally, we think of communication as the transmission and reception of information by means of speech, writing, or other representations of language. Maturana and Varela (1992) portray communication as an internal process that is socially constructed. Habermas (1990) argues that communication of this nature involves a conversational standard where participants actively expose moralistic norms about which they "ought to do" in the attempt to navigate what they "will do." In the conversation between Connie and Joan, Joan was at the point of discovering several things. First, she may be learning to recognize what she doesn't know, in this case school-based instances of racism. Second, she has become aware that discussions about issues related to diversity engender within her deep feelings that she has ignored. Third, and most importantly, she had the opportunity to learn about the experiences of others in her school community.

Most of us are like Joan, in that we experience this inner communication process when encountering an object or a situation that is alien or unfamiliar. Until the alien object or situation is present, these processes are hidden in the background of our consciousness tacitly operating. In Joan's case, it was the seminar on Cultural Proficiency that triggered her internal sense-making process pulling background values, assumptions, and beliefs into foreground operation. In her struggle to understand the experience, she internally processed the information using the most familiar life experience framework available to her. As it is the case for most of us, in these situations, what is said may not be what is heard. Communication depends not only on what is transmitted but also on the internal sense-making process of the person who receives it. To Joan's credit, she courageously reached out to Connie for help in checking her own understanding of what was presented during the Cultural Proficiency session as well as her own reaction to the presentation.

MODES OF CONVERSING

To better help us to understand the connection between communication/conversation and Cultural Proficiency, we introduce what Senge (1994) identified as four forms of conversation most likely to occur in organizations:

- Raw debate
- Polite discussion
- Skilled discussion
- Dialogue

Each form of conversation has distinct purposes and produces specific results. Knowledge of these distinctions can be important for leaders who are intent on leading their schools or districts toward culturally proficient practices. As you read this section, reflect on the narratives from the previous chapters that struck you in particular ways. You will be able place those narratives at various points along Senge's conversation continuum. To illustrate the four forms of conversation, we continue Joan and Connie's conversation in four alternative scenarios—raw debate, polite discussion, skilled discussion, and dialogue.

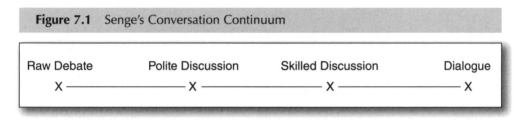

Figure 7.1   Senge's Conversation Continuum

Raw Debate	Polite Discussion	Skilled Discussion	Dialogue
X ——————	X ——————	X ——————	X

Raw debate represents complete advocacy and, although at times polarizing, can identify people's stand on issues. A form of conversation that is rarely helpful in the exploration of issues and ideas is *polite discussion.* Polite discussion, prevalent in schools, is characterized by masking of one's feelings or reactions to issues under consideration. *Skilled discussion* involves a balance of advocacy and inquiry and is most efficient and effective in school settings. *Dialogue,* the opposite of raw debate, involves an intentional discussion in which participants, over time, seek to gain a shared understanding of a topic or issue.

When you review the tables in Chapter 6 or the conversations in Chapter 3, you see examples of these four forms of conversation. As you reread the tables in Chapter 6, from left to right, you will distinguish movement from raw debate to skilled discussion and on to the potential for dialogue.

The four conversation forms, depending on the topic, the purpose, and the situation, are useful in reaching understandings and taking action. To use them effectively, it is helpful to understand both their purpose and their potential outcomes.

Raw Debate. This form of conversation is represented by complete advocacy on the part of each member. Participants hold onto a predetermined position and strategically engage one another. The result is there are declared winners and losers at end of the exchange. This form of conversation can be active or benign. An active form is evident when participants knowingly stake their positions on the issues and relentlessly advocate for their viewpoints. The benign form of debate is evident in hierarchical organizations in which agendas and executive actions forecast predetermined positions and are used to overwhelm opposing ideas. In either case, a power-over dynamic is established, with the winner holding claim to supreme control of the relationship.

If Joan and Connie extend their conversation into active raw debate, it might take this course:

Joan: I have a lot of trouble with that "what are you willing to do, Joan" position! I am willing to become a teacher. I am willing to keep my credential current through professional reading and university coursework. I am willing to come to class prepared. My question is, "Why don't their parents care enough to make sure their kids come to school to learn?"

Connie: I think that is a fair question. My question to us, not just to you, is "What is our role in working with the parents?"

Joan: I didn't become an educator to become a social worker! My responsibilities are very clear—to teach!

Connie: Well, it seems to me that you have a very narrow view of our work and that you are unwilling to entertain any reasonable suggestion.

If it continues, this conversation will most likely devolve into a contentious point-counterpoint conversation until a winner is declared or one party relents. Let's see if polite discussion has any promise for Joan and Connie.

Polite discussion. Participants in this form of conversation have an orientation akin to debate. Although they give appearances of agreement, they actually intend discord. They achieve this by masking their positions in an attempt to show politeness, never truly revealing their thinking about the topic. Polite discussions occur in at least two forms. In a face-to-face conversation, polite discussions are often filled with words such as *but, except, only,* and *however.* In this form of conversation participants are careful not to reveal their true values and feelings but rather to participate in a dance of deception. Polite discussion often occurs as another form when people participate in a discussion, not revealing their feelings or opinions, but when encountering their colleagues in the hallways or in parking lots have no difficulty expressing their true reactions. Had Joan and Connie chosen to continue their conversation as a polite discussion, we may have heard something like the following:

Joan: Well, that Cultural Proficiency presentation yesterday certainly was interesting, but . . .

Connie: What do you mean "interesting, but . . ."?

Joan: Oh, it was okay. It's just that when you have been here as long as I have, you learn that every few years some new initiative shows up and a consultant comes in and reminds us of what we need to do to be successful with these kids in our classes. I just check it off my list of "diversity experiences."

Connie:	It sounds like it was a waste of your time.
Joan:	Oh no, I just know the game.
Connie:	The game? I'm not getting your point.
Joan:	Oh, it's nothing in particular. By the way, Connie, tell Dr. Campbell that I'll be glad to serve on any committee she organizes. Tell her she can always count on me!

What do you think? At this point in the conversation, do you think it's likely that Joan is willing to do the deep internal work of integrating the Five Essential Elements of Cultural Competence as standards for her work as an educator? It appears that she is closing herself to that opportunity and politely choosing superficial compliance as her path.

By moving their conversation to the level of skilled discussion, Connie and Joan can have heightened opportunity to use conversation to explore each other's support and resistance to issues related to diversity.

Skilled discussion includes a balance of inquiry and advocacy and is a productive way of conversing. Healthy debate is encouraged with an equal balance of dialogue. Leaders who are effective in skilled discussion balance their conversations by seeking to understand another's perspective. They openly reveal their own position on a topic and seek to understand another's viewpoint through active questioning. They are aware of their own assumptions and beliefs and know how to express them in meetings. They encourage everyone's participation in meetings. They seek to gain multiple perspectives on issues. These leaders guide discussants to critically examine their own beliefs and assumptions.

Joan:	Connie, your comment that "we are not observers, we are participants in the change process" is disconcerting, at best.
Connie:	I'm not sure what you mean, Joan.
Joan:	I've been on the curriculum committee for the past three years. I've been the one to press our colleagues to actively integrate the teaching standards into our daily work. I don't see myself as an observer.
Connie:	On those issues, you are definitely a facilitator and supporter. My comments are about your reaction to the topic of racism. My interest isn't to put you into a corner, but to be responsive to your request for me to listen to your reaction to the Cultural Proficiency presentation. How can I be most helpful to you?
Joan:	Good point! You're doing it by keeping me focused. As difficult as this is, I do appreciate it!

Though this part of the narrative doesn't indicate shared understanding, it does demonstrate the ability to engage relationships that could lead to investigative exchanges around deep educational issues. Both Joan and Connie experience the opportunity to gain an understanding of each other's position on the topic at hand, and they both seek an understanding of each other's feelings and reactions as they emerge in the conversation. Dialogue may provide Connie and Joan the opportunity to take a next step in the process of substantive, deep, enlightening, and effective conversation.

Dialogue is oriented toward inquiry for the purpose of developing a collective understanding of a given topic. A reciprocal power dynamic, participants attempt to bridge perceived or real differences and come to understand each other's viewpoints. They actively seek to uncover underlying assumptions, values, and beliefs that govern action. Thus, participants in dialogue gain information and insight not only about others but also about themselves.

Joan: You know, this topic of racism perplexes the daylights out of me.

Connie: Perplexes?

Joan: As you've noted, I'm resistant to the information and at the same time I'm aware of intense reactions roiling within me. This may blow you away, but I'd like to learn more about racism.

Connie: Where do you think your resistance comes from?

Joan: I am not sure. Maybe from growing up in a community with no diversity, I'm guessing?

Connie: Where did you live?

Joan: We lived in a very popular city, but not the inner city. It was very progressive. But we did not go to certain parts of the city and live away from any major happenings. Don't get me wrong—we did do things with other schools from across town at events like football, basketball, and other sports.

Connie: When you think about your early experiences, who comes to mind as the leading voice when you think about not being involved with other groups?

Joan: Hmmmm! I never looked at this topic like this before. This is really powerful.

Connie: Yes, racism evokes strong emotional reactions, most of which are associated with our personal experiences and fears. This is great! You've taken responsibility for your own learning.

In our work, we teach two basic dialogic skills that could contribute to Connie and Joan's dialogic conversation. As illustrated in this latter dialogic scenario, participants discuss with one another the "why" of their beliefs or actions. As Connie and Joan's dialogic group forms, they will share viewpoints about racism, student achievement, and other substantive topics. An important component of their sharing exchange will be to probe one another as to why they react to situations or topic they may be perceived as difficult. To move to a deeper level of understanding, they will ask and respond to questions that begin with the "where," "when," and "who" of the sources of their beliefs and assumptions.

Joan and Connie's dialogic journey will cause them to explore their closely held perspectives, or horizons. Horizon is the scope of vision that one might view from a particular vantage point. The depth of your understanding in a given situation is affected by the width or narrow expanse of your horizon.

> The horizon is the range of vision that includes everything that can be seen from a particular vantage point. Applying this to the thinking mind, we speak of narrowness of horizon, of the possible expansion of horizon, of opening up of new horizons, and so forth. . . . A person who has no horizon does not see far enough hence overvalues what is nearest to him. On the other hand, "to have a horizon" means not being limited to what is nearby but being able to see beyond it. A person who has a horizon knows the relative significance of everything within this horizon, whether it is near or far, great or small. (Gadamer 1991, p. 302)

Connie and Joan will eventually come to a moment were their horizons are fused and both emerge with a broader and deeper understanding about various readings, racism, and, most importantly, a recognition of how their individual belief systems are developing.

Examining one's own beliefs and assumptions is an essential undertaking in becoming culturally proficient. Cultural Proficiency involves, after all, an inward journey in which one increasingly understands his own beliefs and actions and the impact his beliefs and actions have on others. A commitment to the process of dialogue is one way for people to deepen their knowledge of themselves and others. Too often, discussions on issues such as racism, privilege, and entitlement are held in a debate format in which positions become increasingly polarized. The consequence of raw debate is the creation of winners and losers and not the development of understanding. As Freire (1999) states, "Only dialogue truly communicates" (p. 45).

Education is a profession grounded in community. How well we communicate with students, parents, and one another is pivotal to the strength of relationship bonds among diverse populations within our education community. Conversation comprises a set of skills that when practiced, can be improved. The following exercise is a successful process we recommend for your use in leading groups in the appropriate use of the four conversation modes. It is not a time-consuming activity. It can be used as a professional development exercise or in grade-level, department, or school faculty meetings. Once you have conducted the activity with colleagues, it is easy to practice any one, or combination, of skills in future meetings. Culturally proficient leaders, as we have indicated throughout this book, are intentional in their work with colleagues, which is why we commend this activity to your use.

PRACTICING CONVERSATION SKILLS

First, have participants review and discuss the conversation continuum. Then place them in dyads (pairs) for the purpose of beginning a dialogue. Instruct participants to move away from tables, facing their partners. The activity is conducted in three rounds. Each round builds on the preceding rounds to provide scaffolding for participant learning.

Round I, limited to three minutes, is an open discussion in which participants are given no guidelines or rules for their conversation. Participants are to engage in conversation as they might in any usual professional setting. As mentioned earlier, we suggest the topic of conversation to be about *change.*

This round serves two purposes. First, participants warm to the activity. Second, it provides the facilitator with immediate data about how the participants engage in conversation. As they converse, the facilitator listens to the participants' word selection, their tone of voice, and the rhythm of their interaction. All three factors play a major role in a successful conversation. Questions, particularly those beginning with the word *why,* are important indicators of the beginnings of a successful dialogic conversation. A courteous exchange of comments can indicate that the participants are engaged in polite discussion. A fast rhythm with few or no questions asked may indicate a debate is in progress.

At the end of the three minutes, instruct the group to stop all interaction, and provide a general critique of the conversational patterns you have observed. Often in the first round, participants fail to listen to one another: They cut into each other's sentences, advocate for points of view, and fail to negotiate differences. Pursuit of collective understanding seldom occurs in this round. Most groups in this round begin conversation with the rhythm of a debate, which is extremely fast. Encourage them to slow the pace and listen to each other's words.

Round II is a controlled conversation session for which the facilitator sets certain rules. The facilitator suggests the topic for this activity. It is important that the topic be general enough to allow for dialogue to ensue. It is our experience that the topic of *change* usually works well as an initial topic of discussion. *Change* is one of those topics that affect everyone— personally and professionally. It is important that the topic not be one rooted in debate. For example, selecting the emotive topic of *racism* is not advised for groups beginning this process. Difficult topics like racism can be tackled as participants master the various modes of conversation.

Each participant is given 90 seconds to continue discussing the topic of *change* while the partner sits and only listens. Although the speaker is allowed to move freely, overt physical gestures or sounds of agreement or disagreement from the listener are not permitted during this round. The facilitator keeps track of time and signals the appropriate moment when participants switch roles. At the end of the round, the facilitator halts all conversation and initiates a debriefing of the process. A question we find effective to begin the debriefing session is *What are your insights as a result of this exercise?*

Most newcomers to dialogic conversation find this step to be extremely difficult because of old habits of jumping into the conversation without listening to what others have to say. Often participants are startled by what they learn from this round. First, they have difficulty believing how slowly time seems to pass during the allotted 90 seconds. Second, they become aware of their inner voice that wants to rush into the conversation before the other person has finished commenting. For many, it is the first time they are aware of how little they listen to one another because of their unwillingness to silence their inner voice and focus on what others have to offer. For the first time they are aware of their continuous orientation to advocate a point and hold ground rather than becoming involved in inquiry of one another's perspectives on an issue.

Round III participants begin a structured process to learn skills of dialogue. Allow 10 to 12 minutes for this round. Participants are encouraged to ask clusters of three to five "why" questions to uncover the speaker's assumptions and predispositions around the topic. For example, when participants discover that they associate control with the topic of change, they may ask *Why is it necessary to be in control of change?* A second "why" question may be *Why is control important?* A third may be *Why do we need to control the lives of others?*

The second step in this round is for participants to ask *where* and *when* questions of one another. *Where* and *when* questions help participants see themselves at a place in time. Understanding of one's own assumptions and beliefs can be revealed as one reflectively responds to questions such as *Where did I learn that change was good or bad? When in my life did I develop such attitudes? Where (or when) did you get the notion that change is controllable?*

The third step involves asking the question of *Who?* This is extremely powerful. A simple question like *From whom did you learn this?* gives one insight into beliefs and values derived from relationships earlier in one's own life. Identifying these relationships affords participants the opportunity to understand when, where, and from whom their values and beliefs were learned. It has been our experience that participants, upon discovering these *where, when,* and *who* connections, discover that many of their values and behaviors function like unspoken contracts with people important in their earlier lives. This knowledge alone provides people with the opportunity to retain, modify, or replace values and/or beliefs—the ultimate compasses for normative action.

Debrief the three rounds by asking participants these questions:

1. What are the contrasting characteristics of the three rounds of conversation in which you were engaged?

2. What seemed comfortable in each round? What was challenging in each round?

3. How do you compare the third round, dialogue, with the conversations that take place in your school setting?

Bohm (1996), a leading proponent of the benefits of dialogue, indicates that true dialogue occurs when we are willing to invest sufficient time. We know that in our schools, time is precious. Although we don't have unlimited time and other resources for professional development, there are several steps leaders must take. We have found that in a short period, participants can learn to navigate the continuum of conversation well enough to have the *beginnings* of good dialogue on difficult issues like racism, entitlement, and oppression. By understanding how to steer colleagues through the four modes of conversation, leaders are able to use dialogue as a way of gaining understanding of their own and others' attitudes and values about issues of race, ethnicity, class, gender, sexual orientation, language proficiency, and ability.

Educators who understand the bases for their own values can choose to change their behaviors. Similarly, these educators can also examine organizational policies and practices for underlying biases. In the next chapter, we discuss the lab protocol technique for educators to examine their policies and practices.

8 Leading in a Culture of Learning and Transformative Change

Unless there is a reflective and historical dimension to our thinking, it will not change how we reason and how we live out our lives.

—Herda (1999, p. 19)

LEARNING HOW TO BE A CULTURALLY PROFICIENT LEADER

Dr. Sam Brewer had been in meetings throughout the day. Early that morning he met over breakfast with Gary Thompson, Maple View's mayor, and several members of the Chamber of Commerce. They were making final plans for the "grand opening" of the new Boys and Girls Club on Main Street in the East Side area. The city purchased the old Central Market building that had been empty for eight years. Sam had worked hard for the last two years to bring this dream to reality. The club would be a place where students living on the East Side of the city could have access to many of the educational supports and opportunities that students on the West Side take for granted. The club would be a safe afterschool center that would offer tutoring, counseling, a library, a computer workshop for desktop publishing and filmmaking, and a sports gym. Sam had started his day with a great sense of accomplishment, and he was looking forward to the ceremony this weekend.

Following his breakfast meeting, Sam returned to the district office and met with several staff members preparing the district's budget for review by the Board of Education. At this point in the school year, preparing the district's budget was taking a lot of his attention. But now, with those meetings behind him, he had a little quiet time in his office to prepare for his next meeting. In a little less than 30 minutes, he would be meeting with all eight of the district's principals in what they collectively had begun calling the "Leadership Lab Team." He smiled, thinking back to almost eight months ago when the group had decided to meet together each Thursday after school as a district leadership team. The choice to meet as a leadership had been a remarkable decision, and it had evolved out of the Cultural Proficiency seminars they had experienced at the beginning of the school year.

The principals had found that the work of facing up to difficult sociocultural problems in their communities and taking them on was not easy, but the leadership team had made a commitment to tackle the work as a group. Sam had gently but firmly challenged the principals to help their teachers become culturally competent educators as a means of eliminating the achievement gap revealed in their analysis of the disaggregated student performance data. That had been another remarkable benchmark. The principals had intuitively sensed the disparities in achievement among different demographic groups of students; nonetheless, they were startled by the harsh revelations in their data. Sam recalled the unifying and inspiring impact this discovery had had on the group. They did not want those results to be their legacy.

By 3:30 p.m., all eight of the principals arrived at the district office for their weekly gathering. Sam had arranged to have coffee, cold drinks, and fruit ready for the meeting, and as the principals came into the meeting room, they helped themselves to the refreshments. Sam was pleased that everyone arrived on time as usual. Their behavior demonstrated mutual respect and showed that the meeting was important to them. At 4:00 p.m., they were all sitting in a circle ready to begin the leadership lab protocol.

Each week, one of the principals presents an "action-learning case," a description of a diversity or equity-related predicament or dilemma that she or he was struggling with. The case presenter also describes the type of feedback he or she wanted the group to offer—cool, warm, or hot. One of the ground rules of the process disallows giving advice or solutions as feedback. Another rule requires all feedback to be framed as a question rather than a statement. The design of the process intentionally provokes the case presenter to be reflective and analytical rather than solution seeking. The principals know advice giving tends to stop reflective analysis and imposes an external solution. The process generally lasts for an hour with about 30 minutes of discussion following the presentation and feedback.

In their early meetings, the group collaborated to define the structure and framework that would guide their lab process. Their joint goal was ambitious. They committed themselves to become culturally proficient leaders as individuals and as a group. They also pledged to create the conditions in which Cultural Proficiency would inform organizational norms and values in their schools and throughout the district. They agreed that the Cultural Proficiency Conceptual Framework would serve as the support to assess their progress.

The Guiding Principles provided their beginning point in devising core values:

- Culture is a predominant force in people's lives.
- The dominant culture serves people in varying degrees.
- People have both personal identities and group identities.
- Diversity within cultures is vast and significant.
- Each individual and each group has unique cultural values and needs.
- The best of both worlds enhances the capacity for all.
- The family, as defined by each culture, is the primary system of support in the education of children.
- School systems must recognize that marginalized populations have to be at least bicultural and that this status creates a unique set of issues to which the system must be equipped to respond.
- Inherent in cross-cultural interactions are dynamics that must be acknowledged, adjusted to, and accepted.

The Cultural Proficiency Continuum provided opportunity to categorize collected data:

- Destructiveness
- Incapacity
- Blindness
- Precompetence
- Competence
- Proficiency

Today's case presenter is Ed Johnson, principal of Maple View Elementary School. Ed is a young African American male in his second year as principal. His school is one of the state's "targeted" schools, meaning that students are not achieving "adequate yearly progress" and are "underperforming." Through his analysis of Maple View's student performance data, Ed has discovered that African American boys are consistently the lowest performing demographic group in all reading skill subtests. Ed has discussed these performance results with several literacy researchers at regional universities, and he has committed to a new research-based instructional process that is showing dramatic results with African American male students. Ed reviewed the research with Sam and, then, with several teachers interested in learning the new instructional strategies. Ed's dilemma is that three veteran teachers who are not involved in implementing the new approach are quite negative and critical of the approach and have generated concern and resistance among African American parents in the community. The parents are demanding that their children not be involved in this "experiment."

The lab protocol (see Table 8.1) provided 15 minutes for Ed to present the case description. A three-minute period followed and was designated as a clarification question and answer opportunity. During this period, Ed is permitted to answer clarifying questions with added information; however, advice couched as questions is not permitted. The next 10-minute period is allocated to the listeners to use for discussion among themselves and planning of feedback they will offer Ed. Ed can observe and listen to the discussion, but he cannot join them. Lab rules require all feedback to be framed as questions intended to provide Ed with reflection and inquiry opportunity about culturally proficient leadership behaviors to support and inform his actions. In the next five-minute segment of the protocol, members of the group offer Ed feedback as questions. Protocol rules call for Ed to listen but not respond to the feedback. One member of the group records the questions so that Ed may consider them more deeply after the meeting. The final phase of the protocol permits Ed an opportunity to reflectively respond to the process. This is not a time to be defensive but to truly consider how his thinking might be challenged by the questions posed by colleagues.

Table 8.1 Learning Lab Protocol

Roles

- **Time Keeper**—keeps track and notifies group about time
- **Recorder**—captures feedback requested by presenter; records feedback
- **Reporter**—leads feedback sharing
- **Presenter**—presents case to the group
- **Listeners**—attends to presenter and provides warm and cool feedback

Presenter prepares a two-page maximum, double-spaced informational abstract of the case for each group member addressing the following elements:

- Name
- School, Department/Grade Level, and Position
- Cultural Proficiency tool focus area
- Purpose—Why are you addressing this topic? What is the importance?
- Summary—Provide an overall summary of the case. Present any artifacts, data, and so on.
- Significance—What is the impact or potential impact?

Presentation

Expanding on the written abstract, presenter gives an oral presentation about actions taken. Listeners prepare to give warm and cool feedback relative to feedback desired by the presenter. When using one of the Cultural Proficiency rubrics, listeners may refer to language and illustrations from the selected rubric.

Listeners silently read two-page abstract	2 minutes
Oral presentation (share artifacts as appropriate) • Explain why I chose this focus area • Elaborate on purpose • Identify improvement opportunities • Describe action • Reflect on or assess actions • Share results (personally and organizationally) • Propose next steps • Request desired feedback	15 minutes
Listeners pose clarifying questions • Seeks omitted information • Reminder, this is not a time to give advice or get into a discussion	3 minutes
Listeners meet and prepare feedback • Presenter leaves room • Listeners prepare warm and cool feedback about the actions taken	10 minutes
Listeners give warm and cool feedback • Presenter does not respond to feedback	5 minutes
Presenter makes closing remarks Not a time to defend the presentation but to reflect aloud on feedback as intriguing and provocative	2 minutes

Feedback

Listeners share feedback with presenter while the presenter listens silently. Feedback begins with warm feedback, moves on to cool feedback, and then moves back and forth between the two. Feedback is written and is given to the presenter after reflection.

(Continued)

(Continued)

Warm Feedback. Warm feedback includes positive comments about how the actions taken seemed to improve presenter's area of focus. Examples might include the following:

- It appears that you have provided opportunities, through your use of team meeting time, to develop understanding of how cultural diversity affects learning.
- The conversations you have with your staff members have helped you to assess the culture of your school. You have a grasp of the dominant culture of your school and who is underserved within it.
- Your use of language from the Tools of Cultural Proficiency has helped you understand and articulate where your school procedures currently are and where you want them to be in the future.
- The way you helped your team members identify their values and encouraged them to act in accordance will help your teammates walk the talk.
- Your workshops were clearly helpful in building staff capacity to "manage the dynamics of difference" within the work environment.

Cool Feedback. Cool feedback is given in the form of questions. It includes possible disconnects, gaps, or problems. Listeners offer ideas or suggestions for strengthening the actions presented. Examples include the following:

- How could you use team meetings to provide opportunities for your colleagues to develop an understanding of how cultural diversity affects learning?
- What steps have you taken to engage students and families to help you assess your school culture?
- How would you use the language of Cultural Proficiency (i.e., Guiding Principles, Continuum, Essential Elements) to describe the office procedures you discussed?
- How have you closed gaps between your team's espoused values and your day-to-day practices?
- How could you build on the success of your professional development sessions to build staff capacity to normalize dialogue, conflict resolution, and problem-solving processes?

Reflection

Presenter speaks to selected feedback comments/questions while listeners are silent.

This is not a time to be defensive; instead, it is a time for the presenter to reflect aloud on those ideas or questions that seemed particularly interesting, intriguing, or provocative enough to advance thinking and action.

After providing considerable warm feedback, the committee provides Ed cool feedback in the form of questions. Talma Moore-Stuart, the principal of Pine Hills High School asked, "Ed, what assumptions do you have about the students that will participate in this new approach? And, what assumptions do you have about their parents?" Ed nods and turns toward Sam who asks, "What information do the parents have about this new approach, Ed? Who have they talked with about it? Why are they calling it experimental?" After a brief pause, Cheryl Robinson, the principal at Greenview Elementary, asks, "When you say professional learning, what specific professional learning outcomes do you want for your teachers in understanding and applying the model? What do teachers know about the research behind the program? Have they talked with the researchers who are promoting this approach or had conversations among themselves to make sense about the concepts?" Then, just as the feedback segment is ending, George Gonzalez, the principal at Main Street Elementary, signals that he has one last question: "Ed, would you put your own kid in this program?" At that moment, everyone looks at Ed as he sits back in his chair. He finishes the protocol with a brief reflection. "Thanks, everybody. You've given me a lot to think about. This has been really helpful and I've got a lot of stuff to process. Thanks." Sam suggests that the group take a brief break and return in 10 minutes for further discussion.

Oscar Medina, the principal at Maple View High School, hands Ed the list of questions he has recorded during the lab process. Ed thanks him and smiles as he tells Oscar, "Wow, I feel like I've had cold water splashed on my face. They're so many things about this new reading approach that I wasn't noticing, and now, I'm more aware of them. Thanks again for the list, Oscar. This will help me focus my thinking."

Ed's perceptions about his dilemma are beginning to shift. The questions that his colleagues have posed in the lab process will help him reconsider and reflectively analyze the situation through the lens of Cultural Proficiency. The action-learning lab process that Dr. Brewer and the Maple View principals use every week offers them a continuing opportunity to participate in a professional culture in which they are developing the confidence and skill to collaboratively question, analyze, and critique their own actions and to give and receive feedback that helps them refocus their leadership behaviors into a repertoire of productive and culturally proficient practices.

The theory guiding use of the action-learning lab is that the knowledge and skills of culturally proficient leadership are complex and require critical reflective inquiry to understand one's own leadership actions. Culturally proficient leadership is not routine, and questions of improving practice are not simple. The structure of the lab process acknowledges the transformative nature of personal, professional, and organizational change necessary to become a culturally proficient leader. Becoming a culturally proficient leader requires an individual to go beyond improving her behavior and to reframe her thinking and alter her perceptions about who she is and the manner in which she and her school serve their school community. The action-learning lab supports such a transformation by engaging participants in progressively deeper and more robust reflection on three personally defining questions:

- Why do I want to be different from who I am now?
- In what ways do I need to be different?
- What will be the indicators to me that I am different?

The five Essential Elements from Chapter 6 are benchmarks for culturally proficient leadership practice. You will recall that the Essential Elements are contextualized as leverage points for change in Chapter 6 and are used to inform personal as well as organizational transformation. In a personal context, leaders use the tables in Chapter 6 to align their personal values and behaviors with the Essential Elements of Culturally Competent behavior. Similarly, the same tables are used to measure progress toward Cultural Proficiency of a school or district's policies and practices.

To realize fully the behaviors implicit in the Essential Elements of Culturally Proficient practice, an individual must develop an awareness or consciousness about her actions as well as the consequences and desired results from those actions. A description of the action-learning lab process that Sam Brewer and the Maple View principals participated in offers an illustration of an educational leader, in this case Ed Johnson, who is becoming increasingly aware of his actions and their consequences. Through the reflective questions posed by his colleagues, Ed was able to become an observer of his own actions, to reflectively analyze his actions, and to begin the process of redefining himself and his role. Ed's example presents a view of transformative learning in action. Through transformative learning experiences like the action-learning lab, practitioners are able to uncover values, assumptions, and beliefs relative to their leadership actions. Emotions and opinions that too often lead to unproductive behaviors are readily clarified. Social relationships like those among the Maple View colleagues provide members opportunities to make sense of and transform their actions in the context of their everyday practice. Continuous examination and reflection on leader actions become habits of practice and organizational norms. As a result, the school district becomes smarter, more effective, and progressively better at redefining itself and its purpose in relationship to the community it serves.

TRANSFORMATIVE LEARNING

Argyris and Schon (1974, 1996) describe patterns of personal and organizational learning on two levels—"single-loop learning" and "double-loop learning." Figure 8.1 displays the relationship between the two patterns. When an individual or an organization's actions result in undesirable or insufficient results, efforts in learning how to improve behavior are a single-loop, reflecting an analysis of one's actions to improve or perform the same actions more effectively. The single-loop pattern refers to the one-dimensional examination and change process. In single-loop learning, an individual does not question the appropriateness or "rightness" of an action or the assumptions from which it derives; the single change made is in the manner in which an individual performs that action.

The double-loop pattern reflects a two-dimensional examination and change process. In double-loop learning, an individual questions the assumptions or frames of reference from which the action emerged; the two levels of change are reshaping ways of thinking and learning to do different things. Thus, the original dysfunctional behavior or action is abandoned in favor of an entirely different way of thinking about the situation, the action, and the desirable result.

Figure 8.1 Double-Loop Learning (adapted from Argyris, 1990, p. 94)

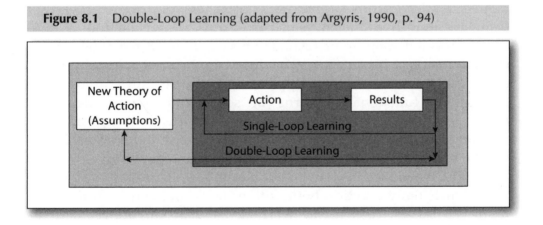

Robert Hargrove (1999) extended the double-loop learning concept to what he calls "triple-loop learning." The triple-loop pattern of learning adds another level of learning by engaging an individual in examining her perception of who she is and what her role or purpose is and transforming that self-image into a new way of seeing herself and her purpose. The key term in this description is "purpose" because the transformative leader values the community they serve. Hargrove describes the triple-loop pattern as "transformational learning" because, as he argues, it is through such learning experiences that an individual fundamentally transforms her way of being and becomes capable of fundamentally different actions. Figure 8.2 shows the triple-loop pattern in relation to the single- and double-loop patterns.

Figure 8.2 Triple-Loop Learning (adapted from Argyris, 1990, p. 94)

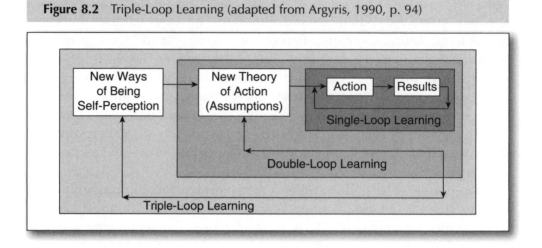

Learning to become a culturally proficient leader requires an individual to go beyond improving his behavior to shifting his perceptions about who he is and what the point of his practice is. In the example of Sam Brewer, Maple View's superintendent, we watch a leader who defines his leadership as culturally proficient practice. His way of being a culturally proficient leader is to display a vision and practice that serves all demographic sectors of his community in equitable fashion. He makes it his purpose to help others become culturally proficient, and he consistently supports leader colleagues in building productive, functional patterns of social interaction. Moreover, Dr. Brewer understands that learning and knowledge transform organizations. Among the principals who participate in the action-learning lab, he has seen individuals make profound changes in how they do their work when they have opportunities to learn within the social context of their daily practice, both within the school and with the community it serves. It is in the learning lab that Dr. Brewer and his administrator colleagues have confronted potentially divisive issues like oppression, entitlement, privilege, and anger and guilt. Similarly, they have practiced skills important to effective conversation and explored personal responsibility and self-determination as alternatives to anger and guilt. The labs provide participants opportunity to explore ways in which to create culturally proficient practices at their schools.

The learning experiences of the lab have reinforced what Dr. Brewer intuitively knew: face-to-face relationships among people in a school are the most powerful influencers of individual learning and change. These evolving relationships are the strongest mechanism for building the organizational knowledge necessary to transform the school's identity, actions, and results. Indeed, researchers studying organizational learning contend that knowledge of new and better practices bubbles up and flows throughout an organization when there is a supportive infrastructure that assumes organizational learning emerges from the inventive, improvisational, and creative ways in which people interact and form relationships (Brown & Duguid, 2000; Brown & Isaacs, 2001; Wenger & Snyder, 2000). Coupling this research with the Tools of Cultural Proficiency (Cross, 1989) offers further, deeper examinations of practice and provokes leaders to analyze their uses of power, privilege, and entitlement to constructively shape a culturally proficient and socially responsible educational organization.

A TRANSFORMATIVE VISION OF MAPLE VIEW SCHOOL DISTRICT

Superintendent Sam Brewer's transformative vision is clear: Maple View School District will exemplify culturally proficient teaching and learning, and every student will achieve academic success. Recall in Chapter 3 how Sam's journey to achieve his vision began with his challenge to the Maple View principals. As he distributed their schools' achievement reports, he pointed out that the results were disaggregated by student demographic groups and he said:

"Look at every demographic group and determine who is doing well and who is not succeeding. Then ask yourselves two questions: 'Why are we getting these results?' and 'Are these the results we want?' It's very important to understand the dynamics in your schools that are producing the results you're getting. Go back and study these results with your teams. Then study your schools. What are your expectations in the relationship you have with each demographic group? Are you meeting those expectations? Why or why not?

"I want each of you to be prepared to describe the obstacles that seem to be getting in the way of student achievement for each demographic group. I also want you to be ready to discuss how the norms for expected behavior, the structures—like scheduling and grouping, the patterns of activity, and the rules and procedures in the school—may be contributing to the obstacles our students are experiencing. I expect each of you to be prepared to describe the obstacles that seem to be getting in the way of student achievement in each group.

"I'm asking you to think about the dynamics of your schools in relation to the principles of Cultural Proficiency that support our district mission. And one other very important thing, I want you to work with your teams to identify five strong values that make your school the school it is."

Sam's call to action for the Maple View principals generated analysis and examination that resulted in an acute awareness of unsuccessful results for some student groups. Unwilling to accept these outcomes as "predictable patterns of failure," Sam envisioned a different future in which every student would achieve success. To achieve his vision required culturally proficient leadership that challenged the people in this school district to change and support them in accomplishing the change. He created the infrastructure, conditions, and opportunities for personal and organizational learning through which knowledge, meaning, and purpose became unified in the goal of being culturally proficient.

GOING DEEPER

In what ways did the information in Chapters 7 and 8 affirm your communication skills? In what ways did the information in these chapters provide new information and skills? How will you use this information in the coming days and months? Please use this space to record your thoughts.

_____

_____

_____

_____

OUR WISH TO YOU AND THE COMMUNITY YOU SERVE

The intent of this book is twofold: to inspire you to take on Sam's challenge as your own personal goal and to provide you with the information and tools to achieve that goal. Culturally proficient leadership happens every day in the choices and decisions an individual makes. When you choose to question your assumptions, change your attitude, and redefine your purpose, you are embarking on a journey of personal transformation. To become culturally proficient, you make the choice to question your assumptions—you face your own anger, guilt, racism, or privilege. Leadership requires you to engage others in facing the challenge of becoming culturally proficient. At its very essence, culturally proficient leadership involves assuming responsibility for challenging and supporting others to question their values, change their perspectives, and develop new ways of behaving when serving historically underserved communities. This view of leadership relies on facilitating learning, knowledge building, and shared commitment to making things better. The choice to lead is yours.

Resources

Book Study Guide

The Culturally Proficient School: An
Implementation Guide for School Leaders

Second Edition

Randall B. Lindsey, Laraine M. Roberts, and
Franklin CampbellJones

Corwin 2013

Chapter 1 Culture Frames Achievement Gaps

Content Questions to Consider

- In what ways do you describe achievement gaps?
- What documented achievement gaps have been identified in your school?
- What do you understand the purpose of this book to be?

Personal Reaction Questions to Consider

- What is your reaction to the intent of this book?
- What is your reaction to examining and discussing access and achievement gaps in your school?

Chapter 2 The Importance of Culturally Proficient Leadership

Content Questions to Consider

- In what ways is Maple View similar to and different from your school or district?
- What did you learn about yourself from the Receptivity Scale?

Personal Reaction Questions to Consider

- What is your reaction to the Receptivity Scale?
- In what ways does the Scale affirm or inform how you view yourself?
- What is your reaction, personally or professionally, as you become acquainted with the Tools?
- What more do you want to know/learn about Cultural Proficiency?

Chapter 3 Overcoming Self-Imposed Barriers to Moral Leadership

Content Questions to Consider

- Describe resistance to change and unawareness of the need to adapt as Barriers to Cultural Proficiency.
- Describe entitlement and privilege as functions of systemic oppression.
- In what ways are self-determination and personal responsibility intended to mitigate the effects of systemic oppression?
- Differentiate among transactional, transformational, and transformative leadership.
- What new insights do you have to the Barriers?

Personal Reaction Questions to Consider

- What are your reactions or feeling about the concepts of entitlement and privilege?
- In what ways did the chapter add to your knowledge and understanding of systemic oppression?

Chapter 4 Cultural Proficiency in Practice: The Guiding Principles

Content Questions to Consider

- What are the Guiding Principles of Cultural Proficiency?
- In what ways are the Guiding Principles of importance to educators?
- In what ways are the Guiding Principles important to schools and school districts?
- What new insights do you have to the Guiding Principles?

Personal Reaction Questions to Consider

- In what ways are the core values expressed in the Guiding Principles consistent with how you view yourself as an educator?
- In what ways does this chapter contribute to your knowledge of your values and assumptions about people who are culturally different from you?
- In what ways are the core values consistent with how you view your school?

Chapter 5 The Cultural Proficiency Continuum: Changing the Conversation

Content Questions to Consider

- In what ways is your understanding of the Continuum deepened after reading the chapter?
- Where do you see yourself at different points of the Continuum, depending on which cultural group you are considering? Why do you think the differences exist for you?

Personal Reaction Questions to Consider

- What reactions do you have to the Continuum? How might colleagues and members of the community view your placement along the Continuum? How do you react to the prospect of having such information?
- What are two or three goals you might want to set for learning about cultures in the community served by your school?

Chapter 6 The Essential Elements as Standards for Leadership Behavior

Content Questions to Consider

- Name the five Essential Elements.
- Describe the manner in which the Essential Elements are informed and supported by the Guiding Principles.
- In what ways do the Essential Elements serve as standards for personal and professional behavior?
- In what ways do the Essential Elements serve as standards for organizational policy and practice?
- How might the Essential Elements be useful for you and your school?

Personal Reaction Questions to Consider

- In what ways is Cultural Proficiency a *journey?*
- How might the Tools of Cultural Proficiency increase your effectiveness? What might be next steps for you?

Chapter 7 Conversation: A Skill for the Culturally Proficient Leader

Content Questions to Consider

- Name Senge's four modes of conversation.
- Describe instances of each mode of conversation being present in your school in the recent past.
- In what ways do modes of conversation support educators' personal Cultural Proficiency journey?
- In what ways do modes of conversation support schools' Cultural Proficiency journey?

Personal Reaction Question to Consider

- What were your thoughts and reactions about the material in this chapter? In what ways do your reactions inform your future communication choices?
- In what ways can you and your school use the information from this chapter?

Chapter 8 Leading in a Culture of Learning and Transformative Change

Content Questions to Consider

- Describe the purpose and use of the lab protocol.
- In what ways does the lab protocol support your Cultural Proficiency *journey?*
- Describe how the process in the lab protocol supports thinking and behavior intent on transformative school change.

Personal Reaction Question to Consider

- How do you react to the prospect of being a transformative leader in addition to a transactional and transformational leader?
- What are the indicators that you are willing and able to display the moral bearing required of moral, transformative leaders?

The People of
Maple View

Character	Role
Dr. Jack Bradley	Hospital CEO
Dr. James Harris	Director of Academic Programs, Tri-Cities Community College
Dr. Sam Brewer	Superintendent
Dr. Charles Banks	School improvement coach
Talma Moore-Stuart	Principal, Pine Hills High School (PHHS)
Rob Moore	Teacher, PHHS
Joel Peters	Teacher, PHHS
Rose Diaz-Harris	Vice Principal, Maple View Elementary School (MVES)
Connie Barkley	Third-grade teacher, MVES
Joan Stephens	Fifth-grade teacher, MVES
Dr. Stephanie Barnes	School improvement coach, PHHS
Hector Broom	Assistant Principal, PHHS
Jack Thompson	Science teacher, PHHS
Janice Thompson	School counselor, PHHS
Maxine Parks	English teacher, PHHS
Ed Johnson	Principal, MVES
Janice Ross	Principal, neighboring district
Jim Jones	Physical education teacher/coach, PHHS
Alice Falls	History teacher, PHHS
Dr. Jesse Phillips	Author

Bob Moore	Sixth-grade teacher, Maple View Middle School (MVMS)
Laura Alvarez	Assistant Principal, MVES
Dr. Belinda Jackson	District math specialist
Ella Chapman	Parent, Maple View Arts (MVA)
Gregory Chapman	Parent, MVA
Anh Me Vu	Parent, MVA
Dr. Andrew Ramsey	Facilitator
Dr. Frederick Jackson	Facilitator
Tony Franklin	Principal, Pine Hills Middle School
Dr. Frank Johnson	Educational administration professor, Midland State University (MSU)
Jung Hai	Graduate student, MSU
Jorge Alvarenga	Graduate student, MSU
Dr. Alfredo Crawford	English language acquisition consultant
Ira Robinson	Math teacher, MVMS
Dr. Laura Ruiz	Reading consultant
Anne Browning	District reading consultant
Dorothy Jackson	Teacher, MVES
Maureen Bailey	Principal, Rose Garden Elementary School (RGES)
Maxine Cho	Teacher, RGES
Dr. Connie Hampton	Principal, Maple View High School (MVHS)
Josh Turner	Biology teacher, MVHS
Irene Thompson	Counselor, MVHS
Helene Kim	History teacher, seventh grade, MVMS
Jackie Sims	Social studies teacher, sixth grade, MVMS
Francisco Alvarado	Assistant Principal, MVMS
Lucy Tyrell	Counselor, MVMS
Kwame Randolph	Parent, MVMS
Sarah Chainey	Science teacher, sixth grade, MVMS
Ron Paige	Algebra teacher, eighth grade, MVMS
Jocelyn Donaldson	Language arts teacher, seventh grade, MVMS
Gary Thompson	Mayor, Maple View
Oscar Medina	Principal, MVHS

Breakthrough Questions

Groups and individuals often are "stuck" in their downward spiral of negative, difficult questions that serve as "barriers" to moving forward to improve student learning. Following are the characteristics of "breakthrough questions."

- Use one or more of the Essential Elements in forming the questions.
  - *How might we learn more about the families represented in our schools?*
  - *What might be some of my reactions to the students and their families in my classroom?*

- Use exploratory and plural language.
  - *What might be several ways we can examine our current structures for access in our classrooms and schools?*

- Use positive intentionality.
  - *What data sources might be available to demonstrate that students in communities like ours are being successful?*

- Use language to mediate thinking toward specific (action) student achievement goals.
  - *As we examine our student achievement data, what are the outcomes we hold for students of all demographic groups?*

- Use language that redirects thinking from certainty to curiosity and possibility, from knowing to not knowing?
  - *What are some questions we need to ask ourselves to help our students move forward academically?*

Unproductive questioning:

- Answer is embedded in question:
  - *Have you thought about . . . ?*
  - *Did you think about . . . ?*

- Judgment and blame are suggested by the question:
  - *Did you realize the effect you were having on those students?*

- Question generates pressure and defensiveness:
  - *Why did you do it that way?*

Adapted from: *Culturally Proficient Learning Communities* by Lindsey, Jungwirth, Pahl, & Lindsey. Corwin, 2009. Not to be used without expressed permission of the authors.

TEMPLATE FOR CONSTRUCTING CULTURALLY PROFICIENT BREAKTHROUGH QUESTIONS

Use the following template to generate current barrier comments and questions in your school and community context. Construct breakthrough questions to mediate thinking and support individuals and your organization moving forward to better serve all students.

Barrier questions and/or comments	Prelude/context	Exploratory language to name the content	Essential Element action verb	Redirected toward goal
	Given (y)our mission statement for equity and diversity . . .	what might be some resources we can access to better . . .	. . . demonstrate value for diversity . . .	. . . so we can reach (y)our student achievement goals?
		What might be some strategies . . .	. . . assess . . .	
	As you examine the current demographics,		. . . to manage . . .	
			. . . to adapt . . .	
			. . . institutionalize . . .	

Adapted from: *Culturally Proficient Learning Communities* by Lindsey, Jungwirth, Pahl, & Lindsey. Corwin, 2009. Not to be used without expressed permission of the authors.

OVERCOMING BARRIERS WITH BREAKTHROUGH QUESTIONS

Examine the following barrier questions. Develop breakthrough questions aligned with the Essential Elements of Cultural Proficiency.

Barrier questions	Essential Elements of Cultural Proficiency	Breakthrough Questions
Why does the conversation always have to be about race?	Assessing our cultural knowledge, Valuing diversity, and Managing the dynamics of difference	In what ways might our conversations about race and culture, as they relate to our community, inform us as educators and support all students' achieving at levels higher than ever before?
Why are we held accountable for kids and parents who don't care?	Valuing diversity, Adapting to diversity	What might be some of the assumptions we hold about "those" parents in our community? In what ways do we demonstrate our values for all families?
How can you expect us to do this when we don't have the time, the right materials, and resources? (Some teachers get stipends to do this.)	Managing the dynamics of differences, Institutionalizing cultural knowledge	In what ways might we use the collective resources we do have available to use Cultural Proficiency to examine our current work? In what ways do we manage our own differences around our resources?
What is keeping us from doing this work, especially with our new kids? We've known about these data for a long time!	Adapting to diversity	What might be some structures or procedures in this school that keep us from better serving our students? How are we adapting to our newcomers?
Why can't we just teach everybody the same way? My strategies work for most kids who really want to learn.	Valuing diversity, Assessing cultural knowledge, Adapting to diversity	What are the values we hold for our students? What four questions might you ask, that if you had the answer to, would make all the difference in your African American students' success?
Before we begin this work and use all these resources and time, how do we know this equity stuff will work?	Managing the dynamics of difference, Valuing diversity	In what ways might we explore schools like ours, with kids and families (demographics) like ours, that are successful?

Adapted from: *Culturally Proficient Learning Communities* by Lindsey, Jungwirth, Pahl, & Lindsey. Corwin, 2009. Not to be used without expressed permission of the authors.

Now, it's your turn: Create breakthrough questions for these barrier questions and comments. How might you use the Essential Elements to help you form the stem for the questions?

Barrier Question	Essential Element	Breakthrough Question
Why do we have to use our prep time as PLC planning time? (I need to get better at teaching math to all kids, not any specific group of kids.)		
Math is math! Why can't we teach all kids using the same "good teaching" strategies?		
How can we be expected to teach "project learning" when we have to use class time to teach content standards using the pacing guide?		
How can we use these "high-achieving" strategies with our kids who can't even read at grade level?		
Why aren't my colleagues supporting my work in the SLC/PLC? I volunteered to teach only low-achieving classes, but why are my fellow teachers talking behind my back because I left the advanced group—so now they have to find a new teacher.		
Since all teachers can't teach AP/honors classes, will we be neglecting our "high" students to teach the "low" kids?		
I know I'm a good teacher because I've been recognized as such, but now I'm being asked to be a "leader," so how will I know how what to do in this new role when my colleagues want me to do all the work for them?		
My administrator asked me to do this new work, but didn't tell me how. How can I do it when he and the other teachers won't help me?		

Adapted from: *Culturally Proficient Learning Communities* by Lindsey, Jungwirth, Pahl, & Lindsey. Corwin, 2009. Not to be used without expressed permission of the authors.

Matrix of Cultural Proficiency Books' Essential Questions

Book	Authors	Focus and Essential Questions
Cultural Proficiency: A Manual for School Leaders, 3rd Ed., 2009	Randall B. Lindsey Kikanza Nuri Robins Raymond D. Terrell	This book is an introduction to Cultural Proficiency. The book provides readers with extended discussion of each of the tools and the historical framework for diversity work. • What is Cultural Proficiency? How does Cultural Proficiency differ from other responses to diversity? • In what ways do I incorporate the Tools of Cultural Proficiency into my practice? • How do I use the resources and activities to support professional development? • How do I identify barriers to student learning? • How do the Guiding Principles and Essential Elements support better education for students? • What does the "inside-out" process mean for me as an educator? • How do I foster challenging conversations with colleagues? • How do I extend my own learning?
Culturally Proficient Instruction: A Guide for People Who Teach, 3rd Ed., 2012	Kikanza Nuri Robins Randall B. Lindsey Delores B. Lindsey Raymond D. Terrell	This book focuses on the five Essential Elements and can be helpful to anyone in an instructional role. This book can be used as a workbook for a study group. • What does it mean to be a culturally proficient instructor? • How do I incorporate Cultural Proficiency into a school's learning community processes? • How do we move from "mind set" or "mental model" to a set of practices in our school? • How does my "cultural story" support being effective as an educator with my students? • In what ways might we apply the Maple View Story to our learning community? • In what ways can I integrate the Guiding Principles of Cultural Proficiency with my own values about learning and learners? • In what ways do the Essential Elements as standards inform and support our work with the Common Core State Standards? • How do I foster challenging conversations with colleagues? • How do I extend my own learning?

Book	Authors	Focus and Essential Questions
The Culturally Proficient School: An Implementation Guide for School Leaders, 2nd Ed., 2013	Randall B. Lindsey Laraine M. Roberts Franklin CampbellJones	This book guides the reader to examine their school as a cultural organization and to design and implement approaches to dialogue and inquiry. • In what ways do "Cultural Proficiency" and "school leadership" help me close achievement gaps? • What are the communication skills I need master to support my colleagues when focusing on achievement gap topics? • How do "transactional" and "transformational" changes differ and inform closing achievement gaps in my school/district? • How do I foster challenging conversations with colleagues? • How do I extend my own learning?
Culturally Proficient Coaching: Supporting Educators to Create Equitable Schools, 2007	Delores B. Lindsey Richard S. Martinez Randall B. Lindsey	This book aligns the Essential Elements with Costa and Garmston's Cognitive Coaching model. The book provides coaches, teachers, and administrators a personal guidebook with protocols and maps for conducting conversations that shift thinking in support of all students achieving at levels higher than ever before. • What are the coaching skills I need in working with diverse student populations? • In what ways do the Tools of Cultural Proficiency and Cognitive Coaching's States of Mind support my addressing achievement issues in my school? • How do I foster challenging conversations with colleagues? • How do I extend my own learning?
Culturally Proficient Inquiry: A Lens for Identifying and Examining Educational Gaps, 2008	Randall B. Lindsey Stephanie M. Graham	This book uses protocols for gathering and analyzing student achievement and access data. Rubrics for gathering and analyzing data about educator practices are also presented. A CD accompanies the book for easy downloading and use of the data protocols. • How do we move from the "will" to educate all children to actually developing our "skills" and doing so?

(Continued)

Book	Authors	Focus and Essential Questions
	R. Chris Westphal, Jr. Cynthia L. Jew	• In what ways do we use the various forms of student achievement data to inform educator practice? • In what ways do we use access data (e.g., suspensions, absences, enrollment in special education or gifted classes) to inform school wide practices? • How do we use the four rubrics to inform educator professional development? • How do I foster challenging conversations with colleagues? • How do I extend my own learning?
Culturally Proficient Leadership: The Personal Journey Begins Within, 2009	Raymond D. Terrell Randall B. Lindsey	This book guides the reader through the development of a cultural autobiography as a means to becoming an increasingly effective leader in our diverse society. The book is an effective tool for use by leadership teams. • How did I develop my attitudes about others' cultures? • When I engage in intentional cross-cultural communication, how can I use those experiences to heighten my effectiveness? • In what ways can I grow into being a culturally proficient leader? • How do I foster challenging conversations with colleagues? • How do I extend my own learning?
Culturally Proficient Learning Communities: Confronting Inequity Through Collaborative Curiosity, 2009	Delores B. Lindsey Linda D. Jungwirth Jarvis V.N.C. Pahl Randall B. Lindsey	This book provides readers a lens through which to examine the purpose, the intentions, and the progress of learning communities to which they belong, or wish to develop. School and district leaders are provided protocols, activities, and rubrics to engage in actions focused on the intersection of race, ethnicity, gender, social class, sexual ableness with the disparities in student achievement. • What is necessary for a learning community to become a "culturally proficient learning community?" • What is organizational culture and how do I describe my school's culture in support of equity and access? • What are "curiosity," and "collaborative curiosity" and how do I foster them at my school/district?

Book	Authors	Focus and Essential Questions
		• How will "breakthrough questions" enhance my work as a learning community member and leader? • How do I foster challenging conversations with colleagues? • How do I extend my own learning?
The Cultural Proficiency Journey: Moving Beyond Ethical Barriers Toward Profound School Change, 2010	Franklin CampbellJones Brenda CampbellJones Randall B. Lindsey	This book explores Cultural Proficiency as an ethical construct. It makes transparent the connection between values, assumptions, and beliefs, and observable behavior, making change possible and sustainable. The book is appropriate for book study teams. • In what ways does "moral consciousness" inform and support my role as an educator? • How does a school's "core values" become reflected in assumptions held about students? • What steps do I take to ensure that my school and I understand any low expectations we might have? • How do we recognize that our low expectations serve as ethical barriers? • How do I foster challenging conversations with colleagues? • How do I extend my own learning?
Culturally Proficient Education: An Assets-based Response to Conditions of Poverty, 2010	Randall B. Lindsey Michelle S. Karns Keith Myatt	This book is written for educators to learn how to identify and develop the strengths of students from low-income backgrounds. It is an effective learning community resource to promote reflection and dialogue. • What are "assets" that students bring to school? • How do we operate from an "assets-based" perspective? • What are my and my school's expectations about students from low income and impoverished backgrounds? • How do I foster challenging conversations with colleagues? • How do I extend my own learning?

(Continued)

(Continued)

Book	Authors	Focus and Essential Questions
Culturally Proficient Collaboration: Use and Misuse of School Counselors, 2011	Diana L. Stephens Randall B. Lindsey	This book uses the lens of Cultural Proficiency to frame the American Association of School Counselor's performance standards and Education Trust's Transforming School Counseling Initiative as means for addressing issues of access and equity in schools in collaborative school leadership teams. • How do counselors fit into achievement-related conversations with administrators and teachers? • What is the "new role" for counselors? • How does this "new role" differ from existing views of school counselor? • What is the role of site administrators in this new role of school counselor? • How do I foster challenging conversations with colleagues? • How do I extend my own learning?
A Culturally Proficient Society Begins in School: Leadership for Equity, 2011	Carmella S. Franco Maria G. Ott Darline P. Robles	This book frames the life stories of three superintendents through the lens of Cultural Proficiency. The reader is provided the opportunity to design or modify his or her own leadership for equity plan. • In what ways is the role of school superintendent related to equity issues? • Why is this topic important to me as a superintendent or aspiring superintendent? • What are the leadership characteristics of a Culturally Proficient school superintendent? • How do I foster challenging conversations with colleagues? • How do I extend my own learning?
The Best of Corwin: Equity, 2012	Randall B. Lindsey, Ed.	This edited book provides a range of perspectives of published chapters from prominent authors on topics of equity, access, and diversity. It is designed for use by school study groups. • In what ways do these readings support our professional learning? • How might I use these readings to engage others in learning conversations to support all students learning and all educators educating all students?

Book	Authors	Focus and Essential Questions
Culturally Proficient Practice: Supporting Educators of English Learning Students, 2012	Reyes L. Quezada Delores B. Lindsey Randall B. Lindsey	This book guides readers to apply the five Essential Elements of Cultural Competence to their individual practice and their school's approaches to equity. The book works well for school study groups. • In what ways do I foster support for the education of English learning students? • How can I use action research strategies to inform my practice with English learning students? • In what ways might this book support all educators in our district/school? • How do I foster challenging conversations with colleagues? • How do I extend my own learning?
A Culturally Proficient Response to LGBT Communities, 2013	Randall B. Lindsey Richard Diaz Kikanza Nuri Robins Raymond D. Terrell Delores B. Lindsey	This book guides the reader to understand sexual orientation in a way that provides for the educational needs of all students. The reader explores values, behaviors, policies, and practices that impact lesbian, gay, bisexual, and transgender (LGBT) students, educators, and parents/guardians. • How do I foster support for LGBT colleagues, students, and parents/guardians? • In what ways does our school represent a value for LGBT members? • How can I create a safe environment for all students to learn? • To what extent is my school an environment where it is safe for the adults to be open about their sexual orientation? • How do I reconcile my attitudes toward religion and sexuality with my responsibilities as a PK–12 educator? • How do I foster challenging conversations with colleagues? • How do I extend my own learning?

References and Further Reading

American Recovery and Reinvestment Act of 2009, Pub. L. No. 111–5, 123 Stat. 115 (2009). Retrieved from http://frwebgate.access.gpo.gov/cgi-bin/getdoc.cgi?dbname=111_cong_bills&docid=f:h1enr.txt.pdf.

Argyris, Chris. (1990). *Overcoming organizational defenses: Facilitating organizational learning.* Needham, MA: Allyn & Bacon.

Argyris, Chris, & Schon, Donald A. (1974). *Theory in practice.* San Francisco: Jossey-Bass.

Argyris, Chris, & Schon, Donald A. (1996). *Organizational learning* (Vol. 2). San Francisco: Jossey-Bass.

Banks, James. (1994). *Multiethnic education: Theory and practice.* Needham, MA: Allyn & Bacon.

Banks, James. (1999). *An introduction to multicultural education* (3rd ed.). Needham, MA: Addison-Wesley.

Block, Peter. (2001). *The answer to how is yes.* San Francisco: Berrett-Koehler.

Bohm, David. (1996). *On dialogue.* New York: Routledge.

Bohn, Anita Petra, & Sleeter, Christine E. (2000). Multicultural education and the standards movement: A report from the field. *Kappan, 82*(2), 156–159.

Brown, John Seely, & Duguid, Paul. (2000). *The social life of information.* Cambridge, MA: Harvard Business School Press.

Brown, Juanita S., & Isaacs, David. (2001, June/July). The world café: Living knowledge through conversations that matter. *The Systems Thinker,* 1–5.

Collins, James, & Porras, Jerry. (1997). *Built to last: Successful habits of visionary companies.* New York: Harper.

Costa, Art L., & Garmston, Robert J. (2002). *Cognitive coaching: A foundation for Renaissance schools* (2nd ed.). Norwood, MA: Christopher-Gordon.

Covey, Stephen R. (1989). *The seven habits of highly effective people.* New York: Fireside.

Cross, Terry L. (1989). *Toward a culturally competent system of care.* Washington, DC: Georgetown University Child Development Program, Child and Adolescent Service System Program.

Cross, Terry L., Bazron, Barbara J., Dennis, Karl W., & Isaacs, Mareasa R. (1993). *Toward a culturally competent system of care* (Vol. 2). Washington, DC: Georgetown University Child Development Program, Child and Adolescent Service System Program.

Cummins, Jim. (1990). Empowering minority students. In N. M. Hidalgo, C. L. McDowell, & E. V. Siddle (Eds.), *Facing racism in education.* Cambridge, MA: Harvard University Press.

Delpit, Lisa. (1995). *Other people's children.* New York: New Press.

Elmore, Richard. (2000). *Building a new structure for school leadership.* Washington, DC: Albert Shanker Institute.

Freire, Paolo. (1970). *Pedagogy of the oppressed* (Nyra Bergman Ramos, Trans.). New York: Seabury.

Freire, Paolo. (1987). *Pedagogy of the oppressed.* New York: Continuum.

Freire, Paulo. (1999). *Pedagogy of hope: Reliving pedagogy of the oppressed.* New York: Continuum.

Fullan, Michael. (1991). *The new meaning of educational change.* New York: Teachers College Press.

Fullan, Michael. (2003). *The moral imperative of school leadership.* Thousand Oaks, CA: Corwin.

Fullan, Michael. (2010). *Motion leadership: The skinny on becoming change savvy.* Thousand Oaks, CA: Corwin.

Gadamer, Hans-Georg. (1991). *Truth and method* (2nd ed.). New York: Crossroad.

Gandhi, Mohandas K. (2002). Available at http://sourcesofinsight.com/gandhi-quotes/.

Garcia, Eugene. (1999). *Student cultural diversity: Understanding and meeting the challenge.* Boston: Houghton Mifflin.

Gay, Geneva. (2000). *Culturally responsive teaching: Theory, practice and research.* New York: Teachers College Press.

Giroux, Henry. (1992). *Border crossings: Cultural workers and the politics of education.* New York: Routledge.

Gladwell, Malcolm. (2000). *The tipping point: How little things can make a big difference.* Boston: Little, Brown.

Goleman, Daniel. (1995). *Emotional intelligence.* New York: Bantam.

Gollnick, Donna M., & Chinn, Philip C. (1990). *Multicultural education in a pluralistic society.* Englewood Cliffs, NJ: Prentice Hall.

Gordon, Milton M. (1964). *Assimilation in American life: The role of race, religion, and national origins.* New York: Oxford University Press.

Graham, Stephanie, & Lindsey, Randall B. (2002, March/April). Balance of power. *Leadership,* 20–23.

Habermas, Jurgen. (1990). *Moral consciousness and communicative actions.* Cambridge, MA: MIT Press.

Hargrove, Robert. (1999). *Masterful coaching.* Retrieved from http://www.roberthargrove.com.

Heifetz, Ronald A. (1994). *Leadership without easy answers.* Cambridge, MA: Belknap.

Heifetz, Ron, & Linsky, Martin. (2002). *Leadership on the line: Staying alive through the dangers of leadership.* Cambridge, MA: Harvard Business School Press.

Herda, Ellen A. (1999). *Research conversations and narrative: A critical hermeneutic orientation in participatory inquiry.* Westport, CT: Praeger.

Hilliard, Asa. (1991). Do we have the will to educate all children? *Educational Leadership,* 40(1), 31–36.

hooks, bell. (1990). *Yearning: Race, gender and cultural politics.* Boston: South End Press.

Kovel, Joel. (1984). *White racism: A psychohistory.* New York: Columbia University Press.

Kozol, Jonathan. (2007). *Letters to a young teacher.* New York: Crown Publishers.

Ladson-Billings, Gloria. (1994). *The dreamkeepers: Successful teachers of African-American children.* San Francisco: Jossey-Bass.

Levin, Henry M. (1988). *Accelerated schools for at-risk students.* New Brunswick, NJ: Center for Policy Research in Education.

Lindsey, Delores B., & Daly, Alan J. (2012). Scaling and sustaining cultural proficiency: The case of Wichita public schools. In Honigsfeld, Andrea & Cohan, Audrey, Eds., *Breaking the mold of education for culturally and linguistically diverse students.* New York: Rowan and Littlefield Education.

Lindsey, Delores B., Jungwirth, Linda D., Pahl, Jarvis V.N.C., & Lindsey, Randall B. (2009). *Culturally proficient learning communities: Confronting inequities through collaborative curiosity.* Thousand Oaks, CA: Corwin.

Lindsey, Delores B., Terrell, Raymond D., Nuri Robins, Kikanza., & Lindsey, Randall B. (2010). Focus on assets, overcome barriers. *Leadership, 39*(5), 12–15.

Lindsey, Randall B., Nuri Robins, Kikanza, & Terrell, Raymond D. (1999). *Cultural proficiency: A manual for school leaders.* Thousand Oaks, CA: Corwin.

Lindsey, Randall B., Nuri Robins, Kikanza, & Terrell, Raymond D. (2003). *Cultural proficiency: A manual for school leaders* (2nd ed.). Thousand Oaks, CA: Corwin.

Lindsey, Randall B., Nuri Robins, Kikanza, & Terrell, Raymond D. (2009). *Cultural proficiency: A manual for school leaders* (3rd ed.). Thousand Oaks, CA: Corwin.

Loewen, James W. (1995). *Lies my teacher told me: Everything your American history textbook got wrong.* New York: New Press.

Loewen, James W. (2009). *Teaching what really happened.* New York: Teachers College Press.

Maeroff, Gene. (1999). *Altered destinies: Making life better for school children in need.* New York: St. Martin's.

Maturana, Humberto, & Varela, Francisco. (1992). *The tree of knowledge: The biological roots of human understanding.* Boston: Shambhala.

McCarthy, Cameron. (1993). After the canon: Knowledge and ideological representation in the multicultural discourse on curriculum reform. In C. McCarthy & W. Crichlow (Eds.), *Race identity and representation in education.* New York: Routledge.

Myrdal, Gunnar. (1944). *An American dilemma: The Negro problem and modern democracy.* New York: Pantheon.

National Governors Association Center for Best Practices. (2010). *Common core state standards.* Washington, DC: Council of Chief State School Officers.

Nieto, Sonia. (2000). *Affirming diversity: The sociopolitical context of multicultural education* (3rd ed.). Reading, MA: Addison-Wesley.

Nieto, Sonia. (2004). *Affirming diversity: The sociopolitical context of multicultural education* (3rd ed.). Reading, MA: Addison Wesley.

Nuri Robins, Kikanza, Lindsey, Randall B., Lindsey, Delores B., & Terrell, Raymond D. (2002). *Culturally proficient instruction: A guide for people who teach.* Thousand Oaks, CA: Corwin.

Nuri Robins, Kikanza, Lindsey, Randall B., Lindsey, Delores B., & Terrell, Raymond D. (2012). *Culturally proficient instruction: A guide for people who teach* (3rd ed.). Thousand Oaks, CA: Corwin.

Oakes, Jeannie. (1985). *Keeping track: How schools structure inequality.* New Haven: Yale University Press.

Ogbu, John. (1992). Understanding cultural diversity and learning. *Educational Researcher, 21*(8), 5–14.

Owens, Robert G. (1995). *Organizational behavior in education* (5th ed.). Boston: Allyn & Bacon.

Perie, Marianne, Moran, Rebecca, & Lutkus, Anthony D. (2005). *NAEP 2004 trends in academic progress: Three decades of student performance in reading and mathematics* (NCES 2005–464). Washington, DC: U.S. Department of Education, Institute of Education Sciences, National Center for Education Statistics.

Quezada, Reyes L., Lindsey, Delores B., & Lindsey, Randall B. (2013). *Culturally proficient practice: Supporting educators of English learning students.* Thousand Oaks, CA: Corwin.

Reeves, Douglas B. (2000). *Accountability in action: A blueprint for learning organizations.* Denver, CO: Center for Performance Assessment.

Sadker, Myra, & Sadker, David. (1994). *Failing at fairness: How America's schools cheat girls.* New York: Charles Scribner's Sons.

Sapon-Shevin, Mara. (1993). Gifted education. In L. Weis & M. Fine (Eds.), *Beyond silenced voices: Class, race, and gender in United States schools.* Albany: State University of New York Press.

Schein, Edgar H. (1992). *Organizational culture and leadership.* San Francisco: Jossey-Bass.

Schon, Donald A. (1987). *Educating the reflective practitioner: Toward a new design for teaching and learning in the professions.* San Francisco: Jossey-Bass.

Schwartz, Theodore. (1978). Where is the culture? Personality as the distributive locus of culture. In George D. Spinder (Ed.), *The making of psychological culture* (pp. 419–441). Berkeley: University of California Press.

Scott, Susan. (2004). *Fierce conversations: Achieving success at work & in life, one conversation at a time.* New York: Berkley Books.

Senge, Peter. (1994). *The fifth discipline fieldbook.* New York: Doubleday.

Senge, Peter M., Cambron-McCabe, Nelda H., Lucas, Timothy, Kleiner, Art, Dutton, Janis, et al. (Eds.). (2000). *Schools that learn: A fifth discipline fieldbook for educators, parents, and everyone who cares about education.* NewYork: Doubleday.

Sergiovanni, Thomas J. (1992). *Moral leadership: Getting to the heart of school improvement.* New York: Jossey-Bass.

Sergiovanni, Thomas J. (2001). *Leadership: What's in it for schools?* London: RoutledgeFalmer.

Sheets, Rosa Hernandez. (2000). Advancing the field or taking center stage: The white movement in multicultural education. *Educational Researcher, 29*(9), 15–20.

Shields, Carolyn M. (2010). Transformative leadership: Working for equity in diverse contexts. *Educational Administration Quarterly, 46*(4), 558–589.

Sizer, Theodore. (1985). *Horace's compromise: The dilemma of the American high school.* Boston: Houghton Mifflin.

Slavin, Robert. (1990). *Cooperative learning: theory, research and practice.* Englewood Cliffs, NJ: Prentice Hall.

Sleeter, Christine E., & Grant, Carl A. (1991). Mapping terrains of power: Student cultural knowledge versus classroom knowledge. In C. E. Sleeter (Ed.), *Empowerment through multicultural education.* Albany: State University of New York Press.

Sleeter, Christine E., & Grant, Carl A. (2007). *Making choices for multicultural education: Five approaches to race, class, and gender* (2nd ed.). New York: Macmillan.

Suarez-Orozco, Marcelo M. (1985, May). *Opportunity, family dynamics, and school achievement: The sociocultural context of motivation among recent immigrants from Central America.* Paper presented at the University of California Symposium on Linguistics, Minorities, and Education. In Garcia, Eugene (Ed.). (1999). *Student cultural diversity: Understanding and meeting the challenge* (2nd ed., pp. 45–146). Boston: Houghton Mifflin.

Tatum, Beverly Daniel. (1999). *Why are all the black kids sitting together in the cafeteria?* New York: Basic Books.

Terry, Robert. (1970). *For whites only.* Grand Rapids, MI: Eerdmans.

Weick, Karl E. (1979). *The social psychology of organizing* (2nd ed.). New York: McGraw Hill.

Wenger, Etienne. (1998). *Communities of practice: Learning, meaning, and identity.* Cambridge, UK: Cambridge University Press.

Wenger, Etienne C., & Snyder, W. M. (2000, January/February). Communities of practice: The organizational frontier. *Harvard Business Review,* 139–145.

West, Cornel. (1993). The new cultural politics of difference. In C. McCarthy & W. Crichlow (Eds.), *Race identity and representation in education.* New York: Routledge.

Wheatley, Margaret J. (1992). *Leadership and the new science.* San Francisco: Berrett-Koehler.

Wheatley, Margaret J. (2002). *Turning to one another: Simple conversations to restore hope to the future.* San Francisco: Berrett-Koehler.

Wheelock, Anne. (1992). *Crossing the tracks: How "untracking" can save America's schools.* New York: New Press.

Zander, Benjamin, & Zander, Rosamund Stone. (2000). *The art of possibility: Transforming professional and personal life.* Cambridge, MA: Harvard Business School Press.

Index

Note: Maple View fictional character names are followed by their role in parentheses.

CORWIN

A SAGE Company

The Corwin logo—a raven striding across an open book—represents the union of courage and learning. Corwin is committed to improving education for all learners by publishing books and other professional development resources for those serving the field of PreK–12 education. By providing practical, hands-on materials, Corwin continues to carry out the promise of its motto: **"Helping Educators Do Their Work Better."**